WOMEN UNDER SCRUTINY

AN ANTHOLOGY OF TRUTHS, ESSAYS, POEMS, STORIES & ART

RANDY SUSAN MEYERS

Dear Carolyn
all of us need more kindness!
xo

Edited by
NANCY MACDONALD

BROOKLYN GIRL BOOKS

Women Under Scrutiny is dedicated to the brave women who stand up and tell the ugly, beautiful, frightening, strengthening, and freeing truths from which we hide

"Truth is powerful and it prevails."
Sojourner Truth

CONTENTS

Why Writing Waisted Terrified Me & How it Led to Women Under Scrutiny   xi

Let The Girls Look How They Want   xvii

PART 1

Childhood Sure Can Toughen a Girl   3

1. Worse Than Sticks and Stones? by Kizzy Preston   5
2. To Be Beautiful You Have to Suffer by Liane Kupferberg Carter   9
3. Crayon Girl by Sydney Elliott   13
4. Which of These Does Not Belong? by Sandy Randazzo   17

PART 2

Daughters of Mothers/Mothers of Daughters   23

5. Mothers of Daughters by Linda C. Boberg   25
6. Female Appraisals by Mary Alice Cookson   29
7. Lipstick Lessons by Allison Harvey   33
8. One Mom's Unlovable is Another Man's Fat by Jennifer Kristin Hugus   37
9. Generations of Judgment by Rebecca Miller   41
10. Clothes: A Girdled-in Life by Arlene Schindler   45

PART 3

Mirror/Mirror   51

11. Don't Stop, Hungry, Fortune Cookie, and Vertebrae by Lizz Matthews   53
12. Supposed to Be by Elisabeth Bassin   57
13. Face It: I'm Old by Peggy Gillespie   61
14. My Body, In What Body, and Her Body by Laura L. Hansen   67

15. It Isn't About What I See in the Mirror Bleary-eyed by Bethany Howard   71

16. Reconciliation by A. Brioné Jackson   73

17. My Mysterious Crotch Hairs by Sue Katz   75

18. Shapeshifting by Sheryl Singleton Lynch   77

19. Plucking by Mara Panich-Crouch   79

20. Morning Musings by Andrea Roth-Smith   81

PART 4

Clothes & Masks: So You Think You Know Me?   85

21. Slipping. Sliding. All but Vanished. by Sahar Abdulaziz   87

22. Appreciating My Body at 69 by Kris Alden   93

23. When the Elephant in the Room is You by L.M. Bennett   99

24. Husky Jeans by Catherine Gentry   105

25. Legs: A Short Story by Liz Esse Kahrs   109

PART 5

Judgment Day   115

26. Confessional by Stephanie English   119

27. This is My Body by Kristin Hills   121

28. Record of Wrongs by Kimberly Ann Priest   125

29. Echo by Lauren J. Sharkey   129

30. Dark Bodies by Shoma Webster   133

31. Bleeding While Catholic: Our Lady of Shame by B. Alexander   137

32. Evangelina Contemplates "Prime Space": A Short Story by Dawn Burns   143

33. Influences by Elizabeth Sinclair Cady   149

34. Short Story From a Post-Divorce Memoir: Partners and Other Conundrums by Nell Carroll   153

35. Alumni of Weight Programs by Heather Clift   157

36. So, I'm Fat. I'm Totally OK with That But You Might Not Be by Frances Danger   161

37. Size Zero? Zero Sense by Katya Duft   165

38. Little Girl by Jessica Fultz   169

39. We Need More Rubens by Dedria Humphries   173
40. On Being Proper by E. B. Moore   175
41. Racked by Julie O'Hora   179
42. Hidden Girl by H. L. Rue   181
43. Fat, and An Open Letter to a Bare Razor Blade by Christine Savoy-Johnson   185
44. Thunder Thighs by Kathleen Slauzis   189

PART 6
Grit & Confidence   193
45. Self-indulgent by Shekinah Davis   195
46. Photo by Venus Prado   197
47. If Only by Amy Blanaru   199
48. Babz at the Barre by Babz Clough   203
49. Am I Beautiful Yet? by Gabrielle Condren   207
50. Transition by Susan Merrifield Desrocher   211
51. Discomfort, and Self-Analysis by Ciahna Heck   213
52. Bodily Appreciation on a Mountaintop by Julie Henderson   217
53. This is Your Life: The Story of a Body by Pamela Johnston   219
54. Head to Toe by Barbara Khan   221
55. Overexposed by Nikki McCoy   225
56. Vicious Cycles by Alexandra Mitchell   229
57. Soft by Rae Noble   233
58. Despite the Nose on My Face by Jennifer "Jay" Palumbo   235
59. She by Tianne Pitz   241
60. Yeah, So I'm a Little Afraid of My Scale by Alisa Schindler   243
61. Optics Management by Laurie Vallas   247
62. Remember That Girl? and Perspectives by Hope Vaughn   251
63. Boob Job Regrets: In Appreciation of Your Previously Small Chest by Densie Webb   255
64. Hiding in Plain Sight: A True Story of Weight Loss by Seedy Wilkins   261

65. Power Pouch by Gretchen Yonko   267

Acknowledgments   271
About Randy Susan Meyers   273
About Rosie's Place   279
Notes   281

WHY WRITING WAISTED TERRIFIED ME & HOW IT LED TO WOMEN UNDER SCRUTINY

RANDY SUSAN MEYERS

"When I was 22, I met with some janky manager, and she told me, 'You're never going to work at this weight.' I think I was a size 6 at the time. There is just this weird thing about how we perceive women in this country. I would love to be a part of breaking that down."

—Melissa McCarthy

When I was a child, my mother hid everything sweet and delicious in the large soup pot she kept on top of the tallest cabinet in the kitchen. Thus, my sister and I, at the tender ages of perhaps five and eight, learned to be mountain climbers. (Only recently did I consider that maybe Mom was hiding the cookies from herself as well as us.) So, some of the things I learned from living with my thin, beautiful mother:

 * The many places where food could be hidden, such as the bottom of our hamper.

 * I could hide things better than my mother, who never found my buried cookies. I'd retrieve and cram them in my

mouth (running the faucet to make sure no chewing sounds were heard) before she could find them.

*Nothing devoured fast and furious (while perched on the edge of the tub) can be savored, but even when they barely register, cookies can taste almost-delicious.

*When sugar is the drug you need, you don't need the perfect delivery system. I didn't need a pretty plate—or even a napkin. (When eating in the bathroom, you have a towel right there.)

All of which led to my new novel, *Waisted*, where seven weight-obsessed women chosen for a documentary about women and their bodies—an endeavor that promised healing—find themselves on lockdown at a hardcore reality show run by punishing, fat-shaming filmmakers.

I played with the first line of this book for over a decade: *"Everyone hates a fat woman,"* but I wrote and published four books before I actually used it in *Waisted*. The story screamed in my head, but I kept it locked away because writing it meant facing myself. Writ honest, the novel would have to include tales of self-loathing, hiding food, and scale-terror—no matter my weight—because, for me, no story is worth writing without emotional honesty at the core.

But, before writing this book, I didn't feel ready to hit the personal nadir that delving into issues of women and weight could/would ignite. Hiding from the truth was far more inviting. And yet, *"Everyone hates a fat woman"* wouldn't let go. So, I began. Once embroiled in the story, I wanted to never eat again, and I wanted to eat every minute. I never wanted to look at a scale, and I wanted to weigh myself three times a day. Part of me wanted to continue denying the cruelty we face from ourselves and others, but I also felt the urge to open myself to every loathsome thought I'd ever had about myself and every bit of self-hatred I (and I imagined other women) held.

I reckoned with my mother teaching me to hate anything short of perfection. I remembered and confronted the question she'd ask on almost every phone call: "How's your weight?" as though "my weight" was something separate from me. Like a roly-poly puppy, I dragged behind me. Or a snarling feral bear.

Inhabiting my characters forced me into terrifying introspection. Could I be at peace with my body and choose who I wanted to be? Could my life be other than a reaction to my mother, magazines, and impossible societal standards? Could I stop denying how my weight—whether up or down—controlled me?

My characters are not my family or me—and yet they are. The inner lives, traumas, and history of novelists always flavor their work. I knew my experiences with issues around body image would be baked into *Waisted*, but I didn't want this novel to be my autobiography, just the butter in the story's cookies. Magic happens when that infusion hits just the right notes. Could I come close to balancing truth and imagination?

I knew this novel would incite strong feelings and reactions, in myself and in others, but I still found myself unprepared. Writing this book was a trauma, a blessing, and a ride into my past, and future. Putting out this novel, more than any I've written, might blow up the hidden craziness about my body that I've carried all these years.

America is jaggedly divided on the topic of women's bodies. Being overweight is an excellent/fantastic/satisfactory choice and anyone who says anything but is fat-shaming!! Being fat is awful, will give you diabetes, and kill you—and anyone who thinks otherwise is a fool!!

Some of us are lucky enough to accept our metabolisms, our crooked parts, our curls when we want waterfalls, our pin-straight brown while we long for bouncing blonde waves. Some of us fight tooth and nail to carve ourselves into perfection. And some of us rail against having to change a thing.

I thought facing myself would be the hardest part of writing *Waisted*, but I was wrong. What was wrenching turned out to be discussing my upcoming novel with teenage girls who then shared how their mothers limited every meal, snack, and drink. Heart-breaking was hearing a woman describe how she was forced to do sit-ups while her brothers ate home-baked desserts. A friend whose brothers fought over her dessert portion—because so many nights she wasn't allowed any sweets.

I wrote exaggerated versions of the stories I saw every day—women whipped by impossible expectations. But was I exaggerating by that much?

That's how it was for me writing this book. I opened my eyes and stumbled into memories of an uncle who remarked on my favorite aunt as she lay in a casket—a casket!—him mourning her by saying that she'd once been so beautiful, but look how fat she ended up! Why, she'd been so stunning, he'd had a crush on her! And look at her now!

My aunt who'd suffered through years of dialysis.

Then this uncle cut his eyes on me and told me to watch out.

I remember my lovely grandmother—always warm, always kind—chiding herself for having a piece of cake at her 97th birthday party.

Now I know this:

The truth is the truth: closing my eyes doesn't make it untrue. Whether I weigh myself or not, I weigh the same amount—but the decision to step onto that scale belongs to me.

From now on, when I chose to eat the damn cake, I will enjoy the damn cake.

And I'll never again serve it to myself from the hamper.

Fifteen years of many-sized me, from 2004 to 2019

As I prepared for the launch of *Waisted*, I thought of all the ways women are scrutinized, judged—and often found wanting. I thought about the previous bonus books I've written which connect to themes from my novels—one filled with recipes and another with thoughts of women and money—and knew what the perfect complement to *Waisted* would be.

Thinking of my characters—with whom I'd fallen so deeply in love—I invited women to write about the relationships they have with their bodies, hair, faces and everything else connected to their outward selves, their facades. How they have been treated by the world based on their appearance—or how they have treated others. I wanted to include serious, humorous, brave and most of all, honest, pieces in the form of essays, poems, photos, or art—however each woman best expressed herself.

I put out a broad call, writing that my agent, Stephanie

Abou, and I would select ten winning contributors. In the end, we were rewarded with brilliant responses from all over the United States, from women in their teens onward, representing a fantastic swath of cultures. We received so many incredible entries that I decided to expand the book—way beyond the slim compilation I envisioned, and expanded the project to a full book with ten first place winners and over fifty finalists.

Perhaps the most difficult part of putting *Women Under Scrutiny* together—a job shouldered more by the editor, Nancy MacDonald, than by me—was choosing the proper category for each piece.

An essay that belonged in *Mirror, Mirror,* also fit into *Mothers and Daughters/Daughters & Mothers.* A poem easy to place in *Judgment Day* could comfortably go in the section titled *Grit & Confidence.* As for *Clothes & Masks,* too many of us find that the right place.

In the end, both Nancy and I hope that through categorizing, editing, and presentation, we did right by all the women in *Women Under Scrutiny.* We love this book and every essay, story, poem, photo, and piece of art within, and thank every contributor for sharing her talent, honesty, and hard work.

All profits from Women Under Scrutiny will benefit Rosie's Place in Boston.

Information about the agency follows the essays, stories, poems and art in the book.

LET THE GIRLS LOOK HOW THEY WANT

Jesse Hoots, age 12

PART 1

CHILDHOOD SURE CAN TOUGHEN A GIRL

RANDY SUSAN MEYERS

"An alcoholic father, poverty, my own juvenile diabetes, the limited English my parents spoke—although my mother has become completely bilingual since. All these things intrude on what most people think of as happiness."

—Sonia Sotomayor

How are we marked by childhood? Who could ever count the ways? As children, we absorb; as parents, we make mistakes no matter how hard we try to do right by our children. When we're lucky, we only cause them mild damage.

Particular childhood memories stand out in stunning detail for most of us—and sadly, it's usually the hurtful moments that we remember the most vividly. One of my memories is how much my mother hated my bangs, dismissing them with the awful words I can barely write: *Hitila bangs*—by which she meant that my bangs resembled Hitler's hair.

And we were a Jewish family. And yes, we did make jokes about almost everything—but oh, when a parent goes even a step too far (or, as in this case, a mile) the damage has a long half-life.

Childhood makes you, breaks you, and forms you. For me, the trick was and is always finding the best way to learn and move on.

Now, as a parent and grandparent, I know how tough being good can be.

1 WORSE THAN STICKS AND STONES? BY KIZZY PRESTON

WINNING ENTRY

I was still young enough to be carried in my mother's arms—the weight of me resting on her right hip—the first time I heard the word.

"Aww, look at that pretty fat baby," the nameless woman said to my mother as she reached up to caress my pudgy cheeks. My mother took a step back, not allowing the woman's hand to actually connect with my face.

"She's not fat...she's healthy," my mother said, defending me and alerting me to what must have been a backhanded compliment, at the same time.

That same "compliment" would follow me from then on with adults constantly wanting to "pinch those fat cheeks" or "give that fat baby a kiss." Soon those comments gave way to criticisms that didn't bother to wear a disguise.

"Do you want a cookie?" my babysitter asked one day, while my mother was at work.

"Yes. Thank you," I said, taking the cookie with glee. Throughout the day, the babysitter continued to offer me snacks, and I continued to accept.

"Your child almost ate me out of house and home today," my babysitter said to my mother, once she came to pick me up that evening. "She just ate constantly."

But she offered, I thought, but dared not speak up, knowing better than to insert myself into "grown folks business."

Apparently, the babysitter waited all day for me to decline her food offers. I never did. We were playing a game that I wasn't aware of and had inadvertently lost.

From then on, keenly aware of my size—bigger than other girls my age—I compared myself to every other girl I came in contact with. Did they leave food on their plates at meal time? Did they say, "No" when it was their turn to play the food offer game? Did boys think they were prettier? Teachers think they were smarter and more talented?

My weight became the lens through which I viewed the world, and the world viewed me. It has felt like people responded to my weight, and not me, whenever I entered a room. Even now.

I don't know if I will ever fix the relationship that I have with my body. I am aware, however, that the negative words regarding my weight from other people—including those closest to me—have meshed into one loud negative force in my own mind that I do battle with daily.

Because of this, I am cautious with my words when I speak to children. I am careful not to say the very same seemingly innocent, yet damaging, comments that were said to me as a child. I fill my words with love and praise, hoping to uplift rather than destroy.

If only I could silence the negative voice in my own mind and replace it with one filled with words of love and accep-tance. Even if I never got thin, at least I would be at peace.

Kizzy Preston is a writer and adult literacy advocate. She earned a Master's degree in Communication, and a Master's degree in Professional Writing from Southern New Hampshire University, and Chatham University respectively. Her writing has appeared on fastweb.com, monstercollege.com, *and* back2college.com, *amongst others. She is working on her first novel.*

2 TO BE BEAUTIFUL YOU HAVE TO SUFFER BY LIANE KUPFERBERG CARTER

I was dragged to Ruth Skaller's Ballet Studio for Girls the year I was seven. I had never expressed any interest in dancing. But earlier that year, I'd had surgery on my eyes, and someone suggested that dancing might help my coordination.

Ruth Skaller was a tall, olive-skinned woman of indeterminate age, whose classes were filled with giggling girls she whipped into line with the snap of her voice. Through a series of barre exercises, we would sweep our Capezio slippers over the polished pale wood floors, *plié, rond de jambe, relevé*, to the strains of haunting, melancholy piano music on the Victrola that only years later would I recognize as Chopin. Mrs. Skater would stand before the mirror, chin cupped thoughtfully in her hand, humming as she turned out muscled legs beneath her skirt drapery as she choreographed our next steps. We would line up, and then, like drifting dandelion fluff—or lumbering elephants—cross the room on the diagonal, spinning and spotting, pirouetting our way dizzily across the studio.

Often the next class would arrive while ours was in progress. Taller, lankier girls would perch on the painted radiators, or sweep into the dressing room behind the studio, a gray affair of cubbies and wrought iron bars over narrow dusty windows that faced an unpaved alley. Swinging rectangular black plastic ballet boxes with pink Barbie-faced ballerinas painted on the front, they would click open the vinyl snaps to remove leotard and tights, then open cunning spaces at the bottom which concealed the soft shoes, or, for the lucky ones, pale pink satin toe shoes with wooden toe blocks.

"Your daughter has promise. She dances with her head," Mrs. Skaller told my mother.

Still, it was three years before I graduated to toe shoes. My mother took me to buy the coveted pink slippers to which she sewed satin ribbons, and a box of pristine lamb's wool, from which I pulled a small cloud to wrap around my toes. At our first toe class, I inserted my stocking-clad foot gingerly into the blocky shoe. Then, standing, I leaned in over a foot to lace the satin ribbons. "No crisscrossed calves, keep that ribbon *low*," Mrs. Skaller warned. And then, like self-important ducks, we girls pigeon-toed out of the dark dressing room into the mirrored brightness of the studio, amidst the brimming eyes of mothers, to take our place at the barre. Awkward and proud, I grimaced in surprise. Lambswool or not, this *hurt*. The familiar steps felt suddenly strange and graceless. Twice in the course of that year, I cracked my large toenail halfway down, and could not dance.

"Art is pain," Mrs. Skaller said, echoing my mother, who, when I flinched as she combed and braided my hair, would say, "To be beautiful you have to suffer."

Still, ballet class was a safe place. Warm, cozy, predictable, a place I carried within me. Controlled and yet free, I seemed to dance from some center of my being, a place which, if I'd been asked to locate, would have made me point to my solar plexus. I elongated my arms, stretched my neck, and fluttered fluid fingers. An enchanted swan. A sugar plum fairy. Giselle. My body could move any way I wished, it was mine to bid, and I was powerful. In my head, I danced all the time. It kept the unnamed, free-floating dread at bay. I could escape the sad and scary thoughts that kept me awake long into the night. My cousin Ruthie's fatal heart defect. My mother's longing for her mother, for whom I was named, who had died young of that unmentionable illness, breast cancer. My other grandmother with the amputated leg, balancing on crutches to bake hundreds of *hamantashen*, who died the same day as her daughter, my Aunt Frances. It was a decade of death. It is not surprising that I was an anxious child. All that was held at bay when I danced. My great aunts and uncles would arrive, and I'd push back the furniture and dance. I dressed my compliant three-year-old brother in blond braids and tutu, forcing him to dance with me. He galumphed loyally. *Swan Lake. The Nutcracker. Dance of the Hours. Gaité Parisienne.* I cast him in my shows, Mickey Rooney to my Judy Garland.

"She's my strongest dancer," Ruth Skaller told my mother, so for the recital she paired me with Rhonda, the large, sweet, but clumsy, girl whose pink leotard billowed in doughy rolls around her middle. While I wore a dainty teal-colored, satin-skirted costume and long, black lace gloves with cut away fingers, Rhonda, tall, stooped and miserable, was made to wear a gold lame tuxedo with tails and tricorn hat. Slow and stolid, her hands sweating, she twirled with me across an auditorium stage to the third movement of Mozart's *Eine Kleine Nacht Musik*.

My body began to change and swell. At eleven, I grew shameful breasts, and hid them beneath an undershirt. "She's 'developing,'" an elderly relative said pointedly at Thanksgiving, and I hated her and wanted to flee. I was humiliated when the bulge of a sanitary napkin showed through my leotard. A month before my twelfth birthday, Mrs. Skaller pulled a tape measure around my waist, fitting me for a costume. She clicked her tongue. "You're putting on weight," she said, and slapped my thigh. Like Rhonda.

I stopped dancing. A swan had become an ugly duckling. I suffered, not for beauty, not for art, but for the betrayal of my body.

Liane Kupferberg Carter is a nationally known writer, journalist and advocate for the autism community. Her work has been published in the New York Times, Washington Post, *and* New York Magazine. *She is the author of an award-winning memoir,* Ketchup Is My Favorite Vegetable: A Family Grows Up With Autism.

3 CRAYON GIRL BY SYDNEY ELLIOTT

Earlier this week, I sent off one of those DNA kits, searching for answers I knew it would not give me. I often wonder what instincts are wired in me, perhaps as far back as early humans strolling across savannas? I imagine the cells of my body, the neurons, the peptides, gray matter, and atoms sorting through the ancient voices and assessing potential danger based on old and new information. Since I don't remember most of what happened to me, I listen to my body's memory, but how much of this is ancestral? Do I carry the fear of the first girl raped by her father? I think back to a friend's comment about being part of a universal web, strands that shake with the wind, the cries of the captured, and the timeless, careless step of a spider as she makes her way across.

I listened to a podcast about a painter who went to seventeen countries to try to define beauty—to see if there were universal connections or parallels between different cultures. Blue is nearly every culture's choice of color. But the favorite painting? A landscape of the savanna, with water, a clear path, low trees, a variety of scrub and grasses, and birds or evidence of wildlife. He argues that beauty is a product of survival. And this survival, or the visual potential of a place hospitable to thriving, finding food, water, and climate, is wired into the DNA of our earliest ancestors, the first tribes in Africa.

We are drawn to beauty for its offering of potential existence, like the child who sits in her tree house, legs dangling off the edge, the feel of oak bark pressed against a hand, as she watches a run-off stream below, clear water moving over silt and stone, pocked with periwinkles clinging on for dear life, as a heron stalls on the edge. Above her, on the hill, the haunted house remains empty except for her brother who might be watching TV, or throwing his stuffed animals into flames, or other things too horrible to mention. I wish I could, but I would be revealing too many secrets in the world of the living. Some things are better left untouched and beautiful.

Somewhere in a closet is a crayon drawing of a girl in a pink dress, blonde hair, all triangles, a wide black cyclone of a mouth, blood spraying in all directions. Out of her abdomen protrudes a knife, the blade larger than her head, lifting her body to the heavens.

I drew this during a therapy session where, under deep relaxation, my "inner child" illustrated my story using my less dominant hand. Many times I nearly threw it away, but it tells a story I still can't bring myself to look at. I hold onto it as if it were a fingerprint, proof of what happened, something tangible and captured. And yet, it exists only as a drawing. A still life with a gaping mouth, capable of swallowing planets.

Sydney Elliott teaches English at Tillamook Bay Community College on the central Oregon coast. Sydney is the editor of The Community College Humanities Review, *and she also teaches yoga, loves to surf and kayak, sings jazz, and volunteers for the county's search and rescue unit.*

4 WHICH OF THESE DOES NOT BELONG? BY SANDY RANDAZZO

One of my favorite pastimes as a kid was creating fictional worlds. I could spend hours lost in a La La Land of make believe, with nothing to keep me company except a few Barbie dolls and my imagination. I felt most comfortable in this dreamy sphere, protected from reality by a cushy layer of blissful ignorance. But shortly after my twelfth birthday, the bubble burst and I found myself thrust unprepared into the awkward realm of pre-adolescence. I soon realized this junior high landscape was no place for dolls and playing kiddie games and that the goal of my existence had become singular in nature: To fit in. I suddenly felt as if I'd been pictured within one of those multiple-choice quiz questions where you have to pick out the item that does not belong, and it was now up to my peers to determine whether or not I belonged.

In this new reality, where my worthiness seemed to be in the eye of the beholder, it became clear that I didn't measure up. There was no shortage of people willing to point out my deficiencies. I was too short, my teeth were too big for my too-small mouth, my babyish voice was a near match to Mickey

Mouse's high-pitched soprano, and my boobs were incognito as though part of a witness protection program.

I watched with envy as my classmates glided into adolescence like seasoned ballerinas, while my own transition resembled Elaine's herky-jerky dance on *Seinfeld*. I wanted so much to fit into society's cookie-cutter mold of normal development that I began pleading with God to make me look like everyone else my age. I prayed for puberty to hurry up, but all that got me was greasy hair and a severe case of acne, while the rest of my body had yet to catch up.

In the realm of constant comparisons, I had become the thing that was unlike the others. Not only had I concluded that my acceptance was directly linked to my physical appearance, but I had also begun to worry that all these external flaws meant that I was also internally flawed. That my outer wrongness was actually a side effect of an intrinsic inner wrongness, and the only way I could fit in was to keep the real me from ever leaking out. But I didn't know how to do that. I hadn't yet learned how to mask the unsavory qualities that made me who I was. So, I did the next best thing. I made myself as small as I felt. I thought if I became as unobtrusive as possible, people would stop noticing me, as well as my imperfections. And it worked. I began earning labels like "shy" and "quiet" and "introverted"—which were far better than those I felt I deserved: ugly, gross, weird. But as with any trade-off, this one came with repercussions that wouldn't materialize until years later.

Fast forward a decade and this sense of inferiority followed me into adulthood in the form of insecurity and self-doubt. I still looked to others for approval, using their praise and criticism as barometers to gauge whether or not the things I said or did were right. I became masterful in the art of shape-shifting, changing as conditions warranted, in order to please them and prove my worthiness. I hustled for love, trading authenticity for acceptance, and in doing so, continued the process of denying myself until the woman I'd become was such a mishmash of other people's expectations that I no longer recognized her.

The sobering realization that I'd spent most of my life trying to be someone I wasn't resulted in my emotional undoing, like unraveling a haphazardly knit sweater simply by pulling on one loose thread. I spent a few more years trying to hold together that version of myself by mending the tattered parts with equally worn patches, but the fixes only added weight to an already weak foundation and eventually the entire thing fell apart. And because my instinct was still to hide my brokenness, I swept up the pieces and lugged them around, along with an unhealthy amount of regret, resentment, and shame, until, after a series of fortunate decisions, I connected with some amazing women who helped me realize that I didn't have to live that way. I could be my genuine, imperfect self without losing the love and affection of those who truly cared about me.

I wish I could end the story here. I wish I could say that mere belief in the possibility of change was enough to instill in me a swift and magical sense of peace and healing, but the truth is, belief is only the beginning. Belief only scratches the most superficial surface. But nestled inside that tiny seed of belief lies a blossom of hope.

So today, at thirty-eight, while I may still have the tendency to look in the mirror and zero in on the same perceived flaws that tormented me all those years ago (along with many, many new ones) and I may still struggle with occasional feelings of doubt and anxiety that what I do and how I speak and who I am is wrong, I am learning to lean into the discomfort. To not see myself as having traits I'm stuck with, but to view them as unique gifts and opportunities for growth that are mine to own and embrace. And I do have hope. I have hope that I will develop the courage to dig even deeper. I have hope that I will someday uncover the wounded little girl who still cowers beneath the layers of scar tissue. And I have hope that when I find her, I will be able to tell her, confidently and definitively, that she is beautiful, and she is loved. Exactly as she is.

Sandy Randazzo writes from the beautiful state of North Dakota where she resides with her husband and dog and is currently at work on her first novel. Connect with her at www.sandyrandazzo.com where she blogs about the truth she's found in writing fiction, or follow her on Facebook @sandyrandazzoauthor.

PART 2

DAUGHTERS OF
MOTHERS/MOTHERS OF DAUGHTERS

RANDY SUSAN MEYERS

"Mothers subject their daughters to a level of scrutiny people usually reserve for themselves. A mother's gaze is like a magnifying glass held between the sun's rays and kindling. It concentrates the rays of imperfection on her daughter's yearning for approval. The result can be a conflagration—whoosh."

—Deborah Tannen

Vector Image by stournsaeh

I am the daughter of a mother who wanted nothing more than for me to wear a size 6, and the mother of two beautiful daughters—daughters I tried to protect from weight worries. (Of course, I failed.)

Ah, life.

In *Not Becoming My Mother* by Ruth Reichl, she writes of living her life under the thumb of her mother's quirks and enraging mothering mistakes, living her life on "Mim tales"—a trait with which my sister and I can over-identify, having dined, perhaps too long, on a treasure trove of Mom stories. I read Reichl's unearthing of her mother's truth, amazed at her courage in revealing her lack of generosity towards her mother, and her ability to finally find the heroic in her mother.

I was with her every step.

Like Ruth Reichl, I, too, berate myself for not managing to rise above the role of daughter to become a woman and friend to my mother. However, when one grows up with a larger-than-life mother, perhaps that's an impossible goal. Maybe only after death severs a relationship that held us so emotionally hostage are we able to step back and offer perspective.

So, thank you, Mom, for being a role model of friendship, you who offered such a striking portrait of being a loyal companion to so many wonderful women.

Thank you for showing such a flair for beauty.

Thank you for showing us the wonder and fun of work.

For laughing very hard. For always appreciating a good story. For your advice on men. And women. Yes, you were often right. About many things. I can now consider you a hero because you lived your life trying very hard. And I know that now.

5 MOTHERS OF DAUGHTERS BY LINDA C. BOBERG

I'm standing in front of the master bathroom's big mirror, scrutinizing my hair. Not the stuff on top of my head. No, I'm hyper focused on the wiry hair that is shooting out of my eyebrows and the one lone, long hair that is creeping out of my nose. Chin hair, my scourge since I was twelve, has multiplied to the point where I take a razor to my face every day. It's an ongoing battle, not lessened by the fact that these hairs are now white instead of black.

As a teenager, I cried to my mother. "Look at me! Who would want to date me? I look like a man!"

Of course, she'd tell me that I was lovely, that no one noticed, that of course I'd date, but years later, when I kissed her soft cheek, she whispered, "Maybe you should get your whiskers removed. They tickle me."

Sigh.

Someone did date and marry me forty years ago, and he has never mentioned chin, nose, or eyebrow hair. His only critique about hair is of the wings that my sideburns become when they get too long. Yet, my daily ritual of finding and cutting, tweezing, or shaving away excessive hair continues in my sixties.

My daughter knocks on the door, calling out, "Are you naked?" For me, one of seven girls who shared one bathroom, it would not matter if she walked in on me as I stand in bra and panties. But to my child, an only daughter, it matters—she's embarrassed whenever I'm half-dressed.

"Give me a minute," I call back, and then throw on the closest t-shirt. "Okay, I'm good."

"You're sure?" she asks, nervous about seeing her mother in anything less than full dress.

As she enters, I continue plucking out the long white hairs in my left eyebrow. They avoid my tweezers like flies avoid a swatter.

As she watches, I say, "Promise me that when I'm old and in a nursing home, you'll find someone to shave me and keep my nose and eyebrows trimmed."

"Ew. That's so gross, Mom."

"Too true. Ow." I finally get one super long, white hair out of my brow. Examining it, I ask, "How do they grow so long overnight?"

As I grab my razor to attack my chin hairs, my daughter says, "You ought to get laser treatment."

I grimace at the thought of spending hours in the dermatology office, only to emerge with a reddened lip and neck.

Maybe she's right. Maybe I should make an appointment.

"How do you like my lip?" she asks, before I have a chance to tell her that her idea is valid.

As I glance at her, I honestly see no difference. My daughter is beautiful to me—her long, curly hair, expressive eyes, long thin hands (my thick hands repulse me), and shapely, curvy body. But she does not see those things in herself. Over the last twenty-something years, she has worried about the size of her butt, the shape of her boobs, the width of her nose, the length of her eyelashes, and even the shape of her lips. We are both tall, thicker woman. We both have big eyes with long lashes and great, thick hair. We also both focus on the negatives.

Long ago, I got over most of it. As a younger woman it was apparent that pretty, thinner, shorter blonde girls were considered more attractive in American culture. They still are. I developed a habit of thinking, "I can't do anything about what nature has given me." My daughter has not reached that point. Even though I have tried to tell her that we cannot fight Mother Nature on things like how wide our backends are, she has done research on every flaw that she sees in herself. The difference is that she acts on perceived faults, including getting a lip lift so that her top lip looks less like the straight line that she sees. Or, she gets eyelash permanents to make her long lashes curl upward more. She's told me that if she could, she'd get her nose redone. The last procedure is cost-prohibitive since insurance won't cover cosmetic procedures, she can't finance it herself, and the Bank of Dad and Mom is closed for beauty treatment loans.

When we moved to California, it was jolting to see all the people who were changing their looks. Cupid-like lips, raised eyebrows, bigger butts, smaller thighs, blonder hair, darker hair, straighter hair, thinner noses, boobs that were so heavy they could almost make one fall face forward– far too many women here seemed disappointed with the looks given to them at birth. I'm sure part of my daughter's reaction to her own looks is because of the beauty message that is shown in media and what we witness every day in Los Angeles.

I long for her to reach the point where she accepts her body —imperfections and all. How do I get her to do this when I'm still standing in front of a strong magnifying mirror to find and remove one more errant hair from my face? I'm not any more accepting of my looks than my daughter is of hers.

Body discomfort is a normal thing when you're one of seven girls—and it doesn't end as you age! When she isn't worrying about her looks, Linda Catanzaro Boberg advises international students, enjoys hiking and traveling with her husband, being mom to three children, and especially writing romance novels.

6 FEMALE APPRAISALS BY MARY ALICE COOKSON

My initiation into the world of female bodies occurred at middle-school sleepovers. After the lights were turned off and parents were out of earshot, my friends and I would play a game we invented called "Tickle." One girl would lie on the floor in her underwear, blindfolded, with her bare arms and legs outstretched. The rest of us not-yet women would sit around her in a circle, each choosing one of her legs or arms to "tickle." Tickling meant lightly stroking her arm or leg with our fingernails in a gentle up and down or circular motion. After about five minutes, the one she judged best tickler got to be in the center.

Aside from imparting the experience of being touched and learning how each of us liked to be touched, this clandestine (sometimes shame-filled) activity familiarized us with each other's bodies. It also evoked comparisons: Who had the biggest breasts? Whose were the pointiest? Who had the most hair? Who among us would our classmates find most desirable? None of these observations had anything to do with our personalities, only our shapes. That's when I began to realize my body was not just something that enabled me to run fast and jump high. It also had a societal value based solely on aesthetics. At thirteen, I had a flat chest, a rounded belly, a pudgy face, and braces. Judging by the commentary of my peers, I deduced my sexual attractiveness—hence, my value—to be fairly low. It was like being launched onto the stormy sea of puberty in a dinghy while others sailed in majestic schooners.

Long after my braces came off and I had a fully developed woman's body, I still felt like that thirteen-year-old girl inside. The college I attended published a directory referred to as the Freshmen Face Book, which was widely circulated in the dorms and at fraternities. The tiny headshots, supplied by our respective high schools, were starred (or not starred) according to our "hotness." Freshman year, I lived with three female roommates who advised me that the combination of my large cup size on my petite frame was considered hot. I decided it best to view my strengths and weaknesses with a sense of humor—especially when my college boyfriend joked that my bangs and glasses made me look like Ernie Douglas from the TV sitcom, *My Three Sons*, a comment I still find hilarious more than thirty-six years later.

Ever since high school, my weight has tended to fluctuate up or down by about ten pounds. When in a thinner phase, I'd hear: *Wow, have you lost weight? You look good!* When I went up a size, nobody said anything. Gradually, I stopped worrying about it. Then one day, when I was about twenty-two, I went bathing suit shopping with a close friend. To this day, her words in the dressing room still ring in my ears: *You really need to do something about your cellulite.* Cellulite isn't something you can do much about; it's hereditary. Something clicked in my head that day as I also recalled my mother saying to me: *It's a shame you got your grandmother's thighs.* All the positive thinking in the world can't erase *"cellulite...big thighs"* coming from women who were supposed to be my closest allies. From then on, I always made sure to put on shorts or a bathing suit cover-up when walking the beach—a habit I continue to this day.

As the mother of a daughter, I've wrestled with how not to impart negative messages and encourage her to love her body. Not knowing how to do this myself, though, I have fallen miserably short. From about ages thirteen to fifteen, my daughter had serious body image issues. My words to her then were particularly dangerous: *People would kill to look like you.* It was the completely wrong thing to say to someone struggling with an eating disorder, and she's never forgotten my lack of sensitivity. My daughter has her own story to tell about being bullied by other girls and how she got back to maintaining a healthy weight. But to this day, I don't think she sees or accepts her beauty. I wish she could see what I see when I look at her!

At twenty-five, my daughter points out that I frequently give her unwelcome compliments, telling her how nice she looks, when what she needs from me is certainly not an assessment of her looks. Rather, she needs to hear: *You're important! You're worthy! You're loved!* Isn't that what all of us want and need? I think one reason I often pay my daughter and other women compliments is that I want to try and repair some of the damage done to me—and to all of us. However, from now on, I'm going to try to cut down on complimenting people on externals, like telling someone, *I love your hair!,* and instead try to focus on more important things: *That was a kind (brave...wise...) thing you did. ...I admire how you always make people feel...* Maybe if we all give each other consistent, kind, and constructive feedback—and stop making unsolicited body appraisals that can have devastating consequences—the next generation will realize its true worth and summon the power to knock our messed-up culture on its ass. We can only hope!

Mary Alice Cookson is a writer/essayist who enjoys living near the sea and near her two adult children on Boston's North Shore. She has edited family magazines on both the East and West coasts and has worked as a television writer in Los Angeles. She may be contacted at maryalicecookson.wordpress.com

7 LIPSTICK LESSONS BY ALLISON HARVEY

"Mama, why do you wear makeup?"

My mascara wand stops mid-swoosh. I turn to look at my five-year-old daughter. Her blue eyes sparkle with both curiosity and excitement. What do I say? In my head swirl a million things I've heard since I was a girl: "Don't leave your dorm room without makeup. You'll never get in a sorority!" "You're not going like *that,* are you? Go fix your face." "A minute on the lips, a lifetime on the hips!"

I don't want this for her. I don't want her to think that I don't feel pretty without makeup on. Because then where would that leave her? So, I give the only answer I can think of in the moment, "Because I want to look like you, of course!"

She climbs up onto the toilet and stands admiring herself in the mirror. "See your rosy cheeks? And your perfectly pink lips? See how long your eyelashes are? I want mine to look like yours!" She eyes me with suspicion.

Already, she's complained about her "unsightly arm hair," thanks to a commercial that ran on repeat at her grandmother's house on the all-kids' channel. Earlier this year, she requested that her hair be in a "messy bun" to be like the other girls in her gymnastics class. "Why would you want to be like everyone else?" I asked her. She rolled her eyes at me. I wasn't prepared for peer pressure to start before Kindergarten.

Yes, the messages our children get begin early. They're in weight loss commercials aimed at the mothers watching cartoons with their children, and in comments from well-meaning adults about how beautiful a little girl looks in her princess gown with neatly curled hair, (but not covered in mud from conducting science experiments in the backyard). Worst of all, these messages are in dolls marketed directly to our children, like the dolls that were the biggest seller of the Christmas season, whose heads were so disproportionately large to their bodies that, if the same proportions were applied to my daughter, her body would crumple under the weight of her head.

My daughter isn't fragile. She's strong. That's one of the things that makes her beautiful. She's as beautiful with tangled hair and muddy feet as she is in a tutu and pink tights. Her full-bodied laugh is infectious. Her stubbornness (while simultaneously driving me crazy) is envy-inspiring. If only I could be that steadfast in holding onto something.

I am the product of years of comments and experiences from my Southern upbringing. I remember how nerve-wracking it was in high school for my friends who had to go to the weekly "weigh-in" to find out if they were thin enough to dance in the kickline under the Friday night lights (and the frantic binging of an entire gallon of ice cream at the end of the season). I can still see my mother's beautiful face register the sting when her Alzheimer's-stricken father told her, "You'd better get those hips under control or you'll never find a man." (An actual Mississippi beauty queen, she was already married to my father, had three children, and was 102 pounds dripping wet.) I cringe as I catch myself giggling at a crazy Southern idiom ("She's so ugly, she'd scare a hungry dog off a meat wagon!"), always followed by a "Bless her heart." Comments like those were handed down from generation to generation.

As I stand in my bathroom, I realize the ridiculousness of applying concealer, foundation, and blush to cover what's naturally there, but I do it anyway. My husband's voice rings in my ears, "I don't know why you think you need all that stuff. I like you better without any of it." My need to create the perfect facade isn't coming from him. It's coming from the combination of everything that led me to the mirror that day: the need to appear perfect, the desire to avoid comments like, "Are you feeling okay? You look tired?" on the odd day when I forget the mascara. It's coming from my own insecurities—insecurities that I don't want for my daughter.

My daughter is still eyeing me with suspicion. This same girl who insisted I sew pockets onto her skirts so that she'd have somewhere to hold the rocks she'd find on the playground, is now wondering what makes someone beautiful. Am I truthful to her in my answer? Am I really doing this to look like her? Yes, I think—in a way—I am. I'm trying to artificially put on the confidence that she already radiates. I put down my mascara wand and face her. "You, my dear, are a beautiful girl. You are strong and smart and kind. You don't need any of this stuff. You are perfect just as you are. Please don't forget that." And in that moment, I realize that I'm telling this to myself as much as I'm telling it to her.

She smiles. I put away the mascara and turn off the bathroom light. We go out to investigate the first of the spring buds in the cold, sunny late February day. I leave my lipstick upstairs.

Allison Harvey has been a storyteller since she learned to talk. A graduate of Vanderbilt University with degrees in music and English, Allison pursued creative careers in New York and Chicago before settling in the Windy City. After becoming a mother and finding that rehearsals took her away from bedtime lullabies more than she would like, she turned her attention to writing. Her first children's series focuses on a young boy with Autism Spectrum Disorder. Her second children's series explores the life of a spunky tooth fairy. Allison lives in the Chicago area with her husband and four children. You can read more of Allison's essays on her blog through her website, www.allisonharvey.com.

8 ONE MOM'S UNLOVABLE IS ANOTHER MAN'S FAT BY JENNIFER KRISTIN HUGUS

"No man will ever love you through the fat," declares my mother (to my tender, neurotic, impressionable twenty-three-year-old self). She is standing akimbo in the middle of the living room in my first official post-college apartment as I attempt to make myself smaller by shamefully curling up in the fetal position in the northernmost corner of my L-shaped couch. I have not yet learned how to defend myself. This pronouncement is delivered swiftly, following a barrage of castigations pertaining to my "inferior" housekeeping abilities at the discovery of a single soiled fork lying at the base of my kitchen sink (in my otherwise immaculate apartment).

Naturally, my mother is making a direct correlation between my slovenliness and my weight, as contributing factors in my unlovability.

Yes, mother. I am unlovable. You got me!

And lo, all these twenty-five years later (at the tender, equally impressionable, albeit emotionally exhausted age of forty-eight), I can safely say she was right: At least in the 3D, physical-interpersonal, "you're nobody 'til somebody loves you" romantic sense.

I am a forty-eight-year-old virgin.

Not that losing one's virginity and love always go hand-in-hand, but for me, love would be required, or at least, desired for that particular rite of passage. And it has been hammered into my psyche that no one has ever actually **loved** me...or at least thought enough of me to not ghost me following three (or fewer) dates. Call me high maintenance, but said behavior is really kind of a deal breaker...both emotionally and physically.

Rest assured, this is not some ambient pity party (at present), merely an analytical point of fact. All the same, I really wish I could tell you, "I am working on it. It is slowly getting better. I have gotten to the root of why I am the way I am and have been having more success in dating and relating," and/or that I could simply just be one of those women for whom everything seems to magically work out, fairy-tale style, despite her sordid past. But no. To this day, my archetypal "evil stepmother" (who is actually my mother) was right: heretofore and forthwith!

Perhaps it is the fact that I live in L.A., the land of fakery or flakery, narcissism, and disingenuousness...and most importantly, superficiality. Call me hypercritical, but in hindsight, most of my dates really weren't that great anyway. One was a recent (two-week) ex-heroin user and poet, hell-bent on dating a "nice girl" for a change, rather than his current, clingy porn star paramour. Another charming lad who declared me to be the "ultimate catch," arrived at our restaurant admittedly high on LSD, and subsequently looked across the room thirty minutes later, and said, "Oh look, my ex-wife is here!" An hour later, he would be abandoning me at a Santa Monica bus station in order to assuage the post-marital interrogations regarding the nature of our meeting. The most Seinfeldian scenario of all, however, would have to be the millennial who "took it out" in the front seat of his car (ostensibly to "put it in" yours truly). Oy!

Hindsight is 20/20, and I have seen all manner of men come, but mostly go. Many of them have proceeded to have fairly successful relationships with all manner of women who are not the gentle author. (God knows how they managed that, but they did.) And I've seen these women...some of whom are empirically more attractive than yours truly, some less, some (but few) with more heartily robust personalities than the Jennmeister (as it should be well established that we hefty gals truly delight in cultivating our personalities and nurturing sensibilities, such that our bodies might not be so harshly judged). That said, all the women the men ultimately chose, however, appear to have one thing in common: skin and bones. They are all skinny, skinny, some to the point of perceptible anorexia. All the same, as a prominent internet meme once read, I could out-hip and out-boob them all any day!!! They, of course, have some colossal "boobs" of their own now, in the form of boys, while I have the mere privilege of delighting in my own, the ones I've always known and loved, (and ones I assume love me), residing immediately on my chest.

So, somehow, whether empirically true or not, in my experience, men do, indeed, prefer slender women. Whether a happy or unhappy coincidence, none of these inferior creatures have ever "wanted" me. So, by way of personal experience, I don't really have all that much else to go on...

As I write these words, I harken back to some of my first therapy sessions, wherein my counselors constantly bolstered my self-esteem by informing me that not everyone is like my mother, and that I deserved much more love than she was ever capable of bestowing upon me. When you are in your twenties, this concept is beyond comforting, if not, empowering. Surely such a person (of the most un-mom-like kind) is out there, and if so, then what is to stop one from entertaining a corrective emotional experience with such a delightful creature? But this, of course, is predicated on the notion that we live in an idealistic world peopled with denizens who are not so touched in the head by the very fears, frustrations and dilemmas that plague my own mother. Alas, based on my own experience, however, most people are "my mom," in sundry forms. And much to my chagrin, I am probably more similar to my mother than I would even care to admit. All the same, like the dial on a scale that measures one's weight, success in love is a numbers game—the higher the number on the scale, the lower the odds of finding that one needle in the haystack.

At the end of the day, we are all at each other's mercy. We all have our vices and our weaknesses, some merely show up on our bodies more than others. So, it is up to us to sow, if not sew (once said needle has been found) those soul connections in as tightly knit a fashion as we can by way/weigh of setting our own fire or passion in accepting, even loving, our fat!

Jennifer K. Hugus was born at a very young age. Having grown up in Massachusetts, France, and Denmark, she is a noted fan of Asian Cuisine. She studied ballet at the Royal Danish Ballet Theatre and acting at U.S.C. Jennifer would like to be a KID when she grows up!

9 GENERATIONS OF JUDGMENT BY REBECCA MILLER

My grandmother was on a diet almost her whole life. She didn't acknowledge it, but she obsessed about what she ate. At eighty-nine years old, she still had saccharin pills in her coffee, Diet Rite bread, and no dessert. I remember right before she died, I offered her homemade sweet bread, hoping it would give her a little energy and she admitted, "I'm just not hungry anymore." After all those years of needless deprivation, even my self-absorbed, twenty-one-year-old self recognized the sadness of this. I vowed I would be strong, healthy and not ever bother with a bathroom scale.

Twenty-five years later, I was in the pediatrician's office with my daughter. The baggy clothes she had been hiding in for the past few months were in a heap on the floor, and I was staring at the scale, stuck at sixty-four pounds. She was twelve and a half years old.

There is a myriad of factors behind eating disorders, but there is a reason why historically, many more women than men suffer in this way. The physical appearance of women and girls has always been public fodder for discussion. I believed I was strong and healthy, but that didn't keep a drunken young man from calling me fat in front of a crowd of his laughing friends—an incident I remember clearly thirty years later. My grandmother had two brothers, two sons, and a cruel mother. None of them hesitated to make offhand comments about her body size or what she was eating. She didn't have the temperament to challenge them, so she snacked in the kitchen and rarely sat down to enjoy her own cooking. My daughter, on the edge of adolescence, was a loner. Without friends to stand with her, she faltered when middle school bullies aimed their taunts at her.

Living in the world of eating disorders, I realized quickly the true danger of our society's obsession with weight. I already knew movies, books, magazines, TV, music videos, and the internet brazenly assessed women's bodies. But now I had to protect a fragile teenager from the triggers that were everywhere. Women talking about their successes and failures at Weight Watchers made me want to scream. The grocery store's thousands of no carb, fat free, sugarless products with calorie counts displayed, made me want to write scathing letters to the proponents of the latest food fads. For my daughter and others with anorexia, losing a few pounds did not mean her jeans fit more loosely, it meant being admitted to the hospital, hooked to machines, to guard against heart and organ failure. It was so much more serious.

Tethered together by my fear for her health, my daughter and I stumbled through her teenage years moving from treatment centers to therapists to nutritionists. She teetered between crisis and coping. Then, six years in, she found a lifeline. It came in the form of a house, where young women lived together with support from mostly female therapists, and led by a woman who had recovered from an eating disorder years before. The program was good, but more importantly, it was a safe environment—free of judgment and full of women who understood.

My grandmother, born in 1896, didn't have the opportunity to heal as my daughter has. She lived in a man's world where she felt she had to keep her figure until old age stole away her appetite. But why, more than a hundred years later, is her great granddaughter still living in a world that judges women this way?

Rebecca Miller, an attorney and writer, worked as a prosecutor before leaving the courtroom to raise her children. Her essays have been published by WBUR's Cognoscenti and she is currently revising her first novel.

10 CLOTHES: A GIRDLED-IN LIFE BY ARLENE SCHINDLER

My beautiful mother had one of those figures that clothes fit flawlessly. She had a tiny waist and a perfectly heart-shaped behind with thin thighs. Who ever heard of a Jewish woman of Eastern European extraction with a small ass and thin thighs? Never exercised, never dieted. I didn't understand how she was born that way, or how I, a chubby teen, could possibly be related to her. As much as I admired her, Mom's physical perfection tormented me—for decades.

When I was eight years old, Mom took me clothes shopping for school. The trip was my reward for getting to skip third grade, at P.S. 179. As I tried on outfit after outfit, Mom told me they all looked too tight. Then, in response to one outfit, she said, "Let's buy it. It will fit...if you wear a girdle. A girdle," she confided, "will give a smoother line to your clothes and keep your chubbiness from showing."

That day, Mom got me my first girdle. My clothes weren't bought to fit my body; my body was contorted to fit my clothes. None of the subtext was lost on me. This was no optical illusion.

Girdles are a lot smaller than actual bodies. If a city was a girdle, and a country was, say, a woman's behind, wearing a girdle is like stuffing a country into a city.

What a challenge it was. I'd step into it, dance it up to my waist, sort of limboing like my life depended upon it.

That's how I started my day, every day...getting ready for fourth grade.

If this happened today, and not in 1964, this torture might be labeled child abuse or, at the very least, child beauty pageant syndrome. Child Protective Services would be contacted, and years of having Lycra cramp my legs might have been avoided.

Wearing something that tight and hard to get in and out of, I didn't really want to take it off during the day until I could take it ALL OFF, meaning—I don't think I ever went to the bathroom my last three years of elementary school. I was too girdled in to pee, I just held it in.

Then, there was how the girdle made me feel, squeezed into my clothes, uptight. I became quiet and hardly spoke in school...my mind and personality became restrained too.

Over-elasticized, I became one of those shy girls who sat in the corner, tugging at her clothes to keep them smooth. With a petite, girdled-in voice. A tightly controlled, inflexibly molded, tushy-torturing girdled existence, I lived a constrained life... afraid of moving too quickly, nothing rowdy, no dancing. I won't dance, don't ask me.

After a few years of wear and laundering, my girdle got a bit stretched out. I experienced an ounce of freedom, and increased mobility. Yet I still maintained that uptight, girdled posture. But I developed a sense of humor. I was ten. I went to parties. I still didn't dance. Sometimes I might be caught swaying to the music, or occasionally head bopping. Dare I look at a boy? Would he know I was a girdle wearer? Right before pantyhose was invented—I remember this well at the sixth-grade dance—there were garter belts with itchy stockings that didn't feel comfortable or sexy. By seventh grade, there were pointy bras...it all hurt. The architecture of torture.

Then came the unprecedented news—not unlike the tearing down of the Berlin Wall—girls could wear pants to school. Yay, ninth grade. Girdle off, jeans on. Now cool jeans were skin tight. And though I still had to lie down to get them on and zip them up, I felt freer...and comfortable enough to use school restrooms. As teens, girls went to restrooms in twos like swim buddies, for gossip and camaraderie—especially me, since I'd stopped wearing girdles and felt more like one of the girls than a product of my Mom's creation. I was still shy and inhibited, but now I was shy and inhibited in denim.

Years passed. Like my stretched-out girdle that had lost its elasticity, I, too, loosened up with time. Even though I no longer wore one, the girdled life was always on my mind—-and in my drawer.

By fifteen, I didn't fit in juniors, or, as they used to say, "missy" sizes. Food was my best friend and comfort. Desserts soothed away feelings of loneliness and filled me up with something sweet and warm to buffer against the cold that was my Mom. And though I had an overcrowded closet of clothes, I still carried my girdle mentality, as my mother denied my need to wear a size 16 or 18. So, my brimming closet was filled with unworn too-tight 14's, and there was unspoken pressure to eventually squeeze into them. Mom bought me most of the size 14 dresses, these reflecting her more sophisticated style in the hopes that I'd be transformed into a lady, resembling her. I remember one such dress, a turquoise mohair sheath that wouldn't look good on anyone bigger than a pencil. Not only could I not zip it up, but the two sides of the zipper appeared to be in different time zones determined never to meet.

Meanwhile, Mom wore a perfect size 6, from her closetful of designer suits and dresses I envied.

Pressured by Mom into following a new diet every other week—the grapefruit diet, the watermelon diet, and the string bean diet (which gave me so much gas I lost interest in resembling a string bean), I was a poster child for calorie counters, fat shamers, and food kvetches.

A thousand sensible salads would never make me as beautiful as Mom. Years later, when I was forty-three, the instigator of the girdled life died! When my mommy was gone, the smoother lines in my clothes and the smoother lines in my life seemed less important. My clumsy nods for perfection died too. And without her to compare myself to, I became beautiful. Girdle in the garbage. My too-tight life was over—with a far more comfortable rear end. And I felt absolutely free!

Arlene Schindler is an author and speaker with expertise in relationships and dating, sharing humorous tales of women's secrets and desires. Her novel The Last Place She'd Look *is a raucous romp through the hidden sex lives of today's "mature" woman. Follow and contact her at* arleneschindler.com.

PART 3

MIRROR/MIRROR

RANDY SUSAN MEYERS

"Being called ugly and fat and disgusting to look at from the time I could barely understand what the words meant has scarred me so deep inside that I have learned to hunt, stalk, claim, own and defend my own loveliness."

—Margaret Cho

from the Randy Susan Meyers Collection

What is beauty?
How do we choose what is attractive or not?
Why do we care so much?

While those aren't questions that I can answer in a few paragraphs, I do know this:

    * Beauty *and* the opposite of beauty is subjective through-and-through.

    * But that doesn't make life any easier—as we're judged not so much by a jury of our peers, but by a jury of the majority opinion of the world in which we live.

    Girls reach an age—I've seen it repeatedly—where staring into the mirror is almost a part-time job. We form 'mirror faces' and study each feature as thoroughly as Marie Curie worked on science.

    The women in the following essays do us all the greatest of services by sharing the truth that we all carry: sometimes the mirror can become our greatest enemy, and the fury we direct at ourselves can be the most challenging war we ever fight.

11 DON'T STOP, HUNGRY, FORTUNE COOKIE, AND VERTEBRAE BY LIZZ MATTHEWS

WINNING ENTRY

DON'T STOP

You comment on my tenuous body and the sharpness
    of my bones when they stick out of my back
And my shoulder blades stick out like two shark fins so
    that every time I see them I hear that music
    from *Jaws*
My jaw likes to pop out of place at random times
    potentially trying to tell me it doesn't know how to
    eat anymore
Just how to quiver
So maybe my jaw and my intestines should get to know
    each other better
Maybe the common ground will make them a little less
    irritable
When I'm hungry I get even more irritable than my
    intestines but I don't want to eat in fear of gagging
    gaggling, giggling, gurgling, trembling

I can't shake the thoughts but my body shakes for me
    my body aches for me
I want to see the indentions in my back where my ribs
    stick out because they remind me of my self-harm
    scars
I want to see my pants hang on my pelvic bones with a
    space underneath like a bridge for jumping or a
    bridge to a life that is not my own
Because I am not the owner of my body anymore
and looking at it,
looking at it

makes me more skinny-prone
makes me all skin and bone

HUNGRY

Aren't you hungry?
Yes, in fact I am
The problem is that my body won't let me know
Anytime I have a craving I get acid reflux and my body
    tells me I'm just nauseous
Anytime my stomach grumbles it punches itself
    disguised as IBS
Anytime I feel my bones dig into the surface I sit upon
    my body screams I was just born this way
And what was once stored in my mind as nutrients has
    distorted its image to look like poison
"I'm allergic to living," my intestines cry
And in place of hives on my arm it paints self-injurious
    scars
I hate my body, I hate my body

But more than that I hate the pain it puts me through
    when I treat it kindly
I hate the illusion it's painted of beautiful sickness
I hate the fact that it tore me apart but tells me I can't
    live without it
I hate the constant torture that tells me it's my only
    friend
And I hate that I keep coming back despite knowing
    that I shouldn't.

FORTUNE COOKIE

I hate myself
For hating myself
And when I love myself
I hate myself for it

I hate myself
For the way my head works
And it makes my head hurt
When it's split in two

VERTEBRAE

I compare my spine to the wire of a spiral bound
    notebook
Letting my papery skin drape from it
And hang
In an array of dancing sheets

And as the notebook is
Dragged along the surface
Each spiral ring is pulled back and released
Shivering and shaking until
They jump back into place
Vertebrae

Lizz Matthews is a poet from Burlington, North Carolina. She began writing at age 14 to cope with severe mental health issues and to overcome childhood trauma. She has published three compilations of poetry; Boiling Water & Bleeding (2016), Nostalgia & Night Terrors (2017), *and* An Open Passage to Truant Fathers (2018).

12 SUPPOSED TO BE BY ELISABETH BASSIN

At sixteen
I studied
fashion magazines,
beckoned by
mannequin wraiths,
short skirts,
impossible limbs.

I yearned
to dwell
in those pages,
a place where
a girl could
disappear,
become spectral,
free of fear.

At last
I lashed
timbers of a raft,
determined
to cross the sea
between
what I was
supposed to be

and me.

I hungered
to hunger
but no crew
tied me
to the mast,
no one halted
my overboard leap
toward the sirens'
pain and beauty.

Instead, a chorus
of well-wishers
bid me
bon voyage,
leaving me to

my folly.

Elisabeth Bassin is a writer, poet, lawyer, and mother. She won Honorable Mention in the Women's National Book Association 2018 Writing Contest, and her work has appeared in several publications. She holds degrees from Princeton University and Harvard Law School.

13 FACE IT: I'M OLD BY PEGGY GILLESPIE

When I turned sixty, I realized that despite the colorful, gauzy skirts from Nepal that I still wore, I could no longer pretend that I was still just a hippie flower child from the sixties. I was sixty! Impossible. Implausible. But looking in the mirror with increasing shock, irrefutable.

So, in what I described to my friends as a "joke 60th birthday present" to myself, I decided to go to a free consultation with Dr. Truswell. Yes, that's his real name! He's a local plastic surgeon who advertises special evenings for women of "a certain age" to learn all about face lifts, liposuction (I could finally get rid of the flabby stomach that has plagued me for years and caused people to periodically ask if I was pregnant, even after I was fifty) and other "non-invasive" techniques like thermage, which involves boiling the collagen in your face with laser beams and then letting it harden so all your wrinkles shrivel and die.

When I showed up at Dr. Truswell's elegant office suite (picture a huge waiting room with a large bubbling aquarium filled with exotic tropical fish and female staff members who all looked twenty-one), I have to admit I assumed everyone else waiting for their consultations would look terrible, except me. I pictured that Dr. Truswell would see me and be bewildered and stunned that I was even there. I imagined walking into his office and having his mouth open wide to say something like, "Whoa, what are you doing here???" Looking at my questionnaire, he would gasp: "YOU are sixty? That's outrageous! You look so much younger than that. I thought you were in your forties. I'm so sorry, but there's nothing I can do for you. Come back in ten years, or maybe twenty. You look absolutely fabulous for your age."

But what actually happened was radically different.

First, Dr. Truswell's gorgeous wrinkle-free nurse (or was it a teenager doing an internship?) whisked me off to a sterile exam room and pulled my hair back off my head with a horrifically tight headband that immediately cut off all blood flow to my brain. Then, she turned on glaring overhead fluorescent lights and started barking orders to me while clicking away on a digital camera with a HUGE close-up lens.

"TURN LEFT AND LIFT YOUR CHIN TO THE RIGHT.... NOW TURN RIGHT AND PUT YOUR CHIN DOWN TOWARDS YOUR CHEST. PURSE YOUR LIPS AS IF YOU'RE KISSING SOMEONE. NOW SMILE AND TIP YOUR HEAD BACK. WAY, WAY BACK. EXCELLENT!"

When she finally took the headband off and led me into Dr. Truswell's even more luxurious inner sanctum, I was a bit shell-shocked. He was sitting on his buttery-soft leather chair looking intently at a gigantic flat-screened computer monitor where a photograph of me was already blown up really, REALLY big.

To put it mildly, I saw images that I still wish I had never seen. Visions that ten years later continue to haunt me. Wrinkles as deep as the deadly crevasses on the icy paths of Mount

Everest. Pores as "majestic" as the craggy, jagged sandstone walls of the Grand Canyon. I felt like I was in a modern-day version of *The Wizard of Oz*, where I had suddenly turned from a cool hipster into the Wicked Witch of Western Massachusetts.

At this point, Dr. Truswell asked me what I wanted. I said, "I want to look like Angelina Jolie." I had prepared that joke before I came to his clinic. He stared at me like I was completely nuts, and even after I told him that I was just kidding, he kept looking at me with condescension and pity in his eyes. After a long pause, Dr. Truswell sighed loudly and told me: "Peggy, you clearly need a complete and total **RENO-VATION**." Yes, that is the **exact** word he used...one that I previously only associated with upgrading the kitchen cabinets or bathrooms in my 250-year-old farmhouse. "Yes," he continued, "a **TOTAL** renovation of your neck, face, eyes, eyelids, forehead, and...(LONG PAUSE)...your ears."

It was obviously no longer a question of an elective procedure. It was clearly, from his point of view (and now, mine), an emergency surgery!

Using a magic laser drawing tool on the computer images of my face, the doctor showed me exactly how I would look after he "fixed" me. No more chicken neck, no crow's feet, no deep creases from my nose to my lips, no more brownish puffy crinkly bags under my eyes, no more droopy eyelids, no low-hanging earlobes. "And during the same surgery," Dr. Truswell said, "you can also have all of your extra fat," (he referred to it using esoteric medical terminology as a "Spare Tire,") vacuumed away. Forever."

Apparently, I would emerge looking as young as I thought I had looked when I had arrived at his office. I looked quite stunning in his images of me post-imaginary surgery. Maybe not quite Angelina Jolie, but perhaps a touch of Julia Roberts mixed in with Jane Fonda.

Just as he could see the immense relief on my hideously old face when I heard there was a cure for aging, he told me that it would only cost $18,000. Plus another $3000, if I wanted a chin implant. And for a three-in-one deeply discounted price, I could have the liposuction added for a mere $4000. "Think about it," he said, turning the screen towards me with the close-up of one of the actual photographs of me before his computer-generated surgical interventions. Every pore and line was visible from across the room.

I stumbled out of his office in a daze, thinking, "How could I justify spending that kind of money when people everywhere were starving, homeless, living in refugee camps? Cyclones, tornadoes, earthquakes, tsunamis everywhere!" I realized that I could probably save hundreds of lives donating this money to Partners in Health instead. On top of the financial concerns, I practice Buddhist mindfulness meditation, and the core teaching is that we must learn to accept that everything is impermanent. And yet, how could I accept walking around town looking like an ancient crone from some ghastly horror flick? I would frighten children. Surely that wouldn't be a positive way to contribute to my community.

This was a true moral and ethical dilemma. What do you think? Do you believe that Dr. Truswell was just trying to make tons of money off another poor innocent woman who was afraid of aging in this crazy culture that only values youth?

I didn't do it. I decided to accept and celebrate my aging body and face. Well, perhaps not celebrate them, but at least stop comparing myself to those flawless movie stars my age who had decided to have "work done."

Ten years have passed and now I'm seventy. I even let my dyed hair turn gray towards the end of my sixties. But since I did, every time I go to the movies or the dentist or even hire a contractor, everyone asks me, "Senior discount?" When I go to NYC and get on a subway, someone instantly stands up and offers me their precious seat. Though I have to admit that I'm happy to sit down, I stew silently. I take the seat, knowing that despite my inner youthfulness, and the fact that I go to Jazzercise four times a week, on the outside, I'm perceived as just an old woman quickly coming up on her Expiration/Use-by date. I must look like an archeological relic, a mummified, leathery, antique human being who can no longer stand on her own two feet. Oy!

So, my question to you is should I spend my money so I can stand proudly on the A train, looking far younger than I really am? So I can pay extra at the movies, for the sake of vanity? I need to know now, before it's really too late to fix me.

What to do? What to do? Help!!!

Peggy Gillespie is a mother, a journalist, and a performer who recently (age 70) appeared completely naked on-stage in San Francisco and Philadelphia as "Nudie Baby" in Taylor Mac's 24 Decade History of Popular Music! She was shocked that she did this. And delighted. She is also the co-founder/director of a non-profit social justice organization, Family Diversity Projects (www.familydiv.org) which creates traveling photo-text exhibits and books including Love Makes a Family: Portraits of LGBT People and their Families *and* Building Bridges: Portraits of Immigrants and Refugees.

14 MY BODY, IN WHAT BODY, AND HER BODY BY LAURA L. HANSEN

MY BODY

That white line along the baseboard
is my body.

It drifts across the floor
like flour
from a day of baking
like chalk
clapped from a blackboard eraser.

It collects like fine sand
at the margins of the room
—my body, my skin.

All winter I leave myself, my cells,
like finely sifted seeds
in corners, crevices,

and wait
to see what will take root.

When I fail to germinate—
skin cells too old or too dry—
I sweep my bits out
of corners and edges,

vacuum
the used-up layers away,
empty myself into the trash.
Later in the week, a truck
will come by to haul me away.

IN WHAT BODY

For I am bodiless and bright.
—from *A Riddle* by Richard Wilbur

In what body will I live my next life?
Will it be better than this condemned shell,
the fingers torqued down into a constant fist,
pebbled at the knuckles, dry as husk?

In what body will I enter again?
Will I walk into a brightly lit room on long legs,
striding, strong? Or will the next
move even more slowly than this one?

Perhaps I will sneak in under low-hanging branches,
dragging along on scarred knees, a tortoise
or gator, snapping and mean. You
will not recognize me, but I

will sense the past life that forces me
to keep eyes open at all times, that remembers
the feel of water on sixteen-year-old skin,
the tug of the comb through tangled hair.

In the next body, in the next life, if there is one,
will the night still call to me, calm me?
With each passing year I grow more restless,
more bored with myself, more agitated

and more unwilling to try. If I am unable
to tolerate the psoriatic skin, the swollen legs
that bob like pontoon floats in the tub, the hair
that falls away like end-of-season leaves

then what do I do but wait? Is it possible
to sleep away the next years like a bear in winter?
A slumbering life, a next life, a spring and then what?
Perhaps something *bodiless and bright.*

HER BODY

At the edge of her body are nerves,
raw and exposed, that chafe
at the touch of the wind,
the rub of her clothes.

At the edge of her body
are little ganglia of thought,
ones she's allowed to escape
but were better left unsaid.

At the center of her body
is a hard knot of fear,
a sadness that bleeds.
All of her interior life

lives on a raft that drifts
the length of her midriff,
a sea that churns and shifts,
ebbs and pulls.

At the edge of her body are places
she's never explored, small bits of flesh
that saunter off the edge
and plunge into the cluttered air.

—from the book *Déjà vu* by Laura L. Hansen,
Finishing Line Press, 2017

Laura Hansen is the author of two poetry collections, Déjà vu *and* Midnight River, *and three self-published chapbooks.* Midnight River *won the Stevens Poetry Manuscript Competition and was a Midwest Book Awards finalist. Laura lives in her childhood home on the banks of the Mississippi in Central Minnesota.*

15 IT ISN'T ABOUT WHAT I SEE IN THE MIRROR BLEARY-EYED BY BETHANY HOWARD

A yawn tries to wake me up as my feet hit the cool tile in the bathroom.

It goes against everything I want...but I turn the light on anyway.

I turn the shower to hot.

I take off my pajamas and stand in front of the mirror to see how I feel about myself today.

I am a little slow to register my thoughts and feelings, so I stand there for what seems like too long.

I assess the situation. Am I better or worse than yesterday? Do I feel chunky or thin? Do I feel completely out of shape or do I feel like I am making strides towards strong? My eyes check off what body part goes in each column: "It Is What It Is," "Mediocre," or "Must Change."

"You aren't sucking in...(inhale) okay, that is better."

I do a little pivot to check out all the angles...well...

The mean voices get loud and so I turn away from the mirror.

The steam beckons from the shower.

I take one last look. Make one last evaluation. No kind words.

Sigh.

I step into warm.

The steam wakes me and warms my body. The water, heat, and truth hit my skin and begin their work to melt and wash away unkindness and lies. I wash my face and hair and feel the suds run down my curves to my toes. I soften. My legs are strong, ready for the day. My hands rub across my soft belly; the silver, jagged lines serve as reminders. Reminders that I sometimes wish would go away, but my body is unrelenting; it won't let me forget the growing, the stretching.

I note the curves and the dimples and don't attempt to put them in a column. My hands smell like garlic from prepping dinner the night before. I smile. Dinner was good. I look down at my cute feet popping with bright coral nail polish and I watch as the last of the criticism washes down the drain.

I emerge clean...wearing only the knowledge that I am beautiful, capable, and strong.

What's for breakfast?

Bethany Howard writes encouraging, always-based-in-reality words at www.-bethanyhoward.com. She loves chocolate, avocado toast, and laughing with friends and family. She believes that we all can be who we are, right where we are and that often we stand in our own way.

16 RECONCILIATION BY A. BRIONÉ JACKSON

I am meeting up with a lifelong friend today and I'm nervous. The last time we were together, I said some unkind things and as a result our relationship has been strained. Thirty-two years we've been friends, we've seen each other through everything. I feel nervous facing her again after how I treated her. What if she doesn't forgive me? I prepare for our meeting by taking a hot shower. I get out, dry myself off and step out of my humid bathroom. I walk into my room with my head low, afraid to face her. She's waiting for me, right there, naked in the yellow frame of my floor length mirror.

"Please have mercy on me this time, please don't be cruel," she seems to beg of me. I give her a once over, my face twisted in a frown, ready to criticize. I start from the bottom of her feet, one of the areas I hate the most. Large, flat. Not graceful in any way. Not slender, not small and delicate the way society likes. "No wonder they don't want you, no wonder no one does," I say to her, my voice is sharp, angry. I realize that I hate her. I gaze over her naked body, she's fat. She disgusts me. She bears scars from the last time I hurt her. Her dark brown skin has stretch marks and scars from acne. "You disgust me," I tell her, my face is hot and wet with tears. She stares back at me with tears in her eyes. She looks me over, starting from the bottom. Her eyes are assuring, confident even. She touches my thighs and then my belly, full and covered with stretch marks. She touches my breasts, small despite my large frame. She touches my face, scarred from hormonal acne. She runs her finger through the coarse, thick strands of my hair. She smiles at me.

"I forgive you, I love you. To me you are everything." I say to myself.

I was born to a single mother in 1986, she always encouraged self-expression. I get my inspiration from my mama, life experiences, and strong black women writers. Pen to paper, or fingers to a keyboard, writing has helped me grow and establish a stronger relationship with myself.

17 MY MYSTERIOUS CROTCH HAIRS
BY SUE KATZ

Aging is playing havoc with my body. Bumps, lumps, spots, moles, broken blood vessels, and wrinkles are turning up, uninvited, in places both public and private. I've gained rolls of fat, dimpled butt cheeks, a neck that looks increasingly like a Slinky, and big honking breasts that don't suit me. I was paranoid about all the fruit flies that suddenly invaded my house until I realized that in fact they're retinal floaters. And where the hell's all my body hair? Even my eyebrows and underarm pits are sparse. But most mysteriously, why is my crotch hair fleeing to my chin?

Sue Katz's business card identifies her as a "wordsmith and rebel." Her writing has been published on the three continents where she has lived and worked. Her recent fiction books, focusing on the lives of elders, include Lillian's Last Affair and other stories *and* Lillian in Love.

18 SHAPESHIFTING BY SHERYL SINGLETON LYNCH

I have been across the spectrum of body sizes in my lifetime. My weight has ranged from "average" to what medical professionals would describe as "morbidly obese." My feelings about how I look have also run the gamut. Tied into this is a phenomenon I have experienced while looking in the mirror. I call it shapeshifting. Although, as it takes place above the shoulders, it has little to do with my weight.

There is something about a bathroom mirror that causes it. Maybe it's the lighting, or the hour, how I feel and think, as I am preparing to face the day. Most days, when I look at my reflection, I just see myself, my familiar face. But some days, when I turn my gaze to the mirror, the image looking back is fluid; the features almost seem to run together. My reaction is one of revulsion. Those days I can't find anything to like about myself. Which came first—the self-loathing or the image in the mirror?

I am in recovery from an eating disorder. In the process of recovery, I have come to terms with some traits which were not very positive. There have been times in my life when I was downright obnoxious. I'm sure that others were justified in rejecting and avoiding me. I was a pain in the ass. Most addicts, of any type, are. I think it's a good bet that I internalized some of those responses. Every so often, the memory of my past behavior seems to surface and cover me like a caul. I am swimming in my own negativity and I definitely don't like it.

The shapeshifting is less frequent these days. That may have to do with my continuing recovery and ability to maintain a healthy weight. It may also have to do with my choice to stop relaxing my hair and wearing makeup. I am more self-accepting of my natural appearance. These days, people seek me out as opposed to running from me. When I look in the mirror, the woman there is happy to see me. We smile at one another.

Sheryl Singleton Lynch is a poet and personal essayist. Her work has appeared in Poet's Sanctuary, Shooting Star Review, Queens Parent Magazine *and* LifeScribes: The Collective Journal, *among others. Sheryl is the author of* On the Precipice of Caring: Essays from My Experience; Serpentine and Firestruck, *a collection of poems; and* The Gypsy's Dream, *a collection of short stories. Sheryl lives in New York City, is married, and has an adult son on the autism spectrum.*

19 PLUCKING BY MARA PANICH-CROUCH

Hirsute
minor trichotillomania
two hours
in morning sunlight
with coffee and tweezers

Robe falling open on the front porch.

each pull
and release
a satisfying form of fishing
poly-syndromic

resist
resist
resist

Insulin
pluck me out

a string strung
fat like resin on my bones
carnivalesque

bearded lady always lives large
a marvel
Resist expansion
Resist soft fur growing
Resist natural elaboration
enlargement amplification development

Sinew from my chin.

Mara Panich-Crouch is a writer, artist, and bookseller in Missoula, Montana. She holds a BA in Creative Writing and English from Purdue University and completed post-graduate studies at the University of Montana. Her work has been published in CutBank Online, The Missoulian, *and is forthcoming in* Awake in the World, Volume 2.

20 MORNING MUSINGS BY ANDREA ROTH-SMITH

When my alarm went off this morning, I laid in my bed a few extra minutes. I ran my hands over my lumps, bumps and unshaven legs. I grabbed my stomach pouch and traced surgical scars and stretch marks with my fingertips. I went into the bathroom, looked in the mirror at the yet to be covered dark circles, puffy morning eyelids, tiny age spots and imperfections. I inspected my aging and yellowing teeth, all the deepening happiness crevices on my face, and turned my head on a swivel to check out my grey hair that is beginning to turn entirely white in some spots. And do you know what that woman in the mirror staring back at me did? She smiled at me...a deep, broad soulful smile...and then a tear ran down her cheek...because she is deeply grateful, has no regrets and is genuinely happy with who she is...from the inside out.

Andrea Roth is a freelance writer born & raised in Southeastern Pennsylvania. Andrea is known for using her personal experiences to make her writings relatable to her readers. When not writing, Andrea lends her efforts as an activist to a myriad of causes including gender, race & LGBTQ equality.

PART 4

CLOTHES & MASKS: SO YOU THINK YOU KNOW ME?

RANDY SUSAN MEYERS

"To be honest, I used to hate shopping. I rarely left a store without crying, cursing my body, and swearing under my breath at the fashion industry."

—Mary Lambert

Photo by Kireevl

Shopping for clothes can flatten me—or, if the moon and stars line up right, as they occasionally do, I can enjoy the experience. However, as a girl, I would have preferred cleaning the bathroom to clothes shopping with my mother, who rarely approved of the size I wore.

I still remember the process of shopping for a dress for my cousin Gary's bar mitzvah. My mother huffed and puffed with impatience as we flipped through the racks—unwilling to look at the 'larger' sizes, unable to compliment and over-willing to criticize.

We found a dress, one that I might have loved if it hadn't felt like we walked out with the only dress that could/would ever fit me.

Now, I look back at photos of me in the dress in utter shock. I felt fat and ashamed of my body. A body that I'd now worship.

Yes, shopping can suck (and might always), but when we finally determine what we want our clothes, our hair, our faces to say, and what works for us, then life in attire becomes far more comfortable. We all wear life-costumes. The trick is often finding the one that best fits who we are, both body and soul.

from the Randy Susan Meyers Collection

21 SLIPPING. SLIDING. ALL BUT VANISHED. BY SAHAR ABDULAZIZ

WINNING ENTRY

I stand, transfixed, staring into the mirror at a face I no longer recognize, at a body that has housed my soul for fifty-plus years, birthed healthy children, sustained me through illness and healed me from falls, and yet, here we are, she and I, practically strangers—adversaries for most of our co-existence. The light brown eyes glaring back at me are tired, worn, angry, and immeasurably sad. It's been a difficult few months, and I am only now coming to terms with my loss.

On the outside, my body is a pretender, an impostor, a fake. She's worn "*just fine*" like an insignia for so long that only the weathering of time has succeeded in unmasking her...bringing her crashing to her knees. Together, we wallow in heartbreak, she and I, weighted down by the stark realization that our well-worn mask of approval is slipping. Vanishing. Being replaced. I want to beg her for forgiveness, tell her how sorry I am for so many things I've thought and said, but she's not ready to hear it. So instead, I lower my gaze, fighting back the torrent of shame, and blame-filled tears, and the urge to descend into darkness.

I am regretful. I should have defended her—*us*—more.

Thanked her more. Shown her the kindness, courtesy, and generosity I have so easily afforded strangers. The same strangers whose low opinions somehow carried more weight than the body which has protected, nurtured and cared for me through sickness and in health, until eventual death do us part. Instead, I have complained, mocked her legs, her waist, the size of her thighs...the texture of her hair, the shape of her nose. Never content. Never satisfied.

Now time, the greatest of equalizers, has reared its demanding head and stepped in. Neither my body nor my soul has the slightest chance against this eternal warrior. The mask that I so carefully crafted out of expensive lotions, oils, and promise-filled creams is now peeling, slipping, and threatening to expose. All that will remain is the unembellished, plain and simple truth, which, for too long, has waited in the wings to debut.

Age. The wearing away of the outer shell. Skin marked by discernible lines and wounds. I have spent a good portion of my life cringing against the tiger scars of motherhood traversing my belly. Laughed in memory of the childhood injuries that still adorn my knees. Detested the welted disfigurements left over from invasive operations, slicing, dicing, reattaching, and repairing my diseased innards.

Age. The pain within. The body parts slowed by indecipherable aches and inscrutable pains. Even sleep, The Great Escape, has become a commodity now.

However, the hardest, most excruciating, most wrenching pain is the invisibility—the way we older women are sidelined and curbed, relegated to the used bin, treated to an array of aggressive sidebar comments, the less than tolerant stares, and the saccharine, placating smiles, as if the longevity of our made-to-measure masks decides our individual worth as women.

Mine is slipping. Sliding. Disappearing. All but vanished.

All I am left with is the truth. The unembellished, unadorned, bare-simple truth. I'm not ready, nor strong enough to accept the inevitable. I thought I was. I told myself I would be. I lied.

This hurts.

I descend the stairs slowly, deliberately, feeling each step press into the bottom of my tender feet. I limp towards the kitchen to make a cup of tea, ignoring the searing ache in my hip. My long, gray hair, pleated into a braid, rests down my now curving spine. As the water comes to a boil, I lean against the sink, staring out the kitchen window, seeing everything and nothing, and desperate to find my voice. My bony hand lined with veins reaches for a mug, but my fingers somehow twitch and retreat, causing the cup to topple out, and crash to the floor. In frustration, I slam my fist against the counter, causing my skin to swell and bruise immediately. Broken ceramic shards surround me, and all I can think is, *how fitting.*

I have begun to hide, sequester myself away from people, from judgment. Unwilling to tolerate all of the *for her age* comments and wounding clarifications. It's all too messy. I'm barely able to navigate my own life, let alone police theirs–or at least that is what I tell myself.

I drag a broom from the closet and sweep up the mess, holding the handle with my now sore hand. I shrug. What's one more pain to add to the long, and already disruptive list?

In moments, the mess disappears and I am left wondering, will this be my fate? Will I too, fade, becoming little more than a fleeting memory? Have I bought into the hoax of youth so profoundly that I no longer value the strength and herstory of my own footprint? I squeeze my eyes closed, searching again for my voice, taunting her to resurface and save me from myself.

I lower my body into a chair to rest. My emaciated shoulders slumped in defeat...wearied by this ravenous disease. I calculate in my head the energy needed to cajole my stiff limbs forward. The computation feels astronomical, unattainable. But I have no choice. Some things need to get done. Obligations don't care about relapses.

Back up the stairs I go, gripping the banister for dear life, panting after every labored step. I contemplate what to wear, and what if any social canon will shatter should I dare decide to show up clothed precisely how I feel...

Once upstairs, I get ready to shower. I slip my bathrobe off, purposely diverting my gaze from the mirror. I stand under the hot shower, lost in blissful nothingness while the water beats against my sore body until my skin begins to pucker. Done, I towel off. That's when I notice a new bruise forming on my forearm.

I select an outfit that only marginally does more than scream comfort. I put on my mask, tie up my hair, throw on a scarf and head out the door. When I arrive, I am met by familiar faces, conversant questions.

"How are you feeling?" I am asked repeatedly in passing.

Do I dare speak the truth? Tell them that every cell in my body hurts? That when I look at myself in the mirror, I want to cry? That this old, weathered face with the sagging jawline scares me?

"I feel just fine," I reply, in a voice I no longer recognize. Slipping. Sliding. Disappearing. All but vanished.

Sahar Abdulaziz has authored seven books: But You LOOK Just Fine, As One Door Closes, The Broken Half, Secrets That Find Us, Tight Rope, Expendable, *and* Trust. *Abdulaziz's work covers a wide range of hard-hitting topics: mood disorders, domestic violence, marital/family dysfunction, racism, sexism, and prejudice, but most of all—survivorship.*

22 APPRECIATING MY BODY AT 69 BY KRIS ALDEN

Over the past year and a half, I've been pretty much home-bound due to a seemingly never-ending parade of illnesses, surgeries, and hospitalizations. I've had a LOT of time to watch television, read books, peruse magazines and waste way too much time online.

One of the things that has made me insane is the contin-uous hatred and shaming that is directed at girls and women. We are told that we are not beautiful, not worthy, not equal in a variety of hateful and disgusting ways. And, while this misogyny and destructive language is directed at all females, it is particularly vicious when directed at women who have larger bodies who don't fit into society's norm of what qualifies as beauty (read white, young, size 2, and probably blonde). At a time when 57% of all women in the United States are a size 14, this demand for us all to fit into a very tiny box is disturbing and repressive. Girls as young as six are worrying that they look "fat" in a bathing suit. Larger women are cloaking themselves in oversized clothing in the hope that bigger clothes will hide their bodies. Beautiful, strong, powerful bodies.

In my adult life, I've weighed from 123 to 252 pounds. I wasn't happier at the lower weight and I wasn't more depressed at my heaviest. When I was 123 pounds, I desperately wanted to be 110, because I knew that in society, my power came from having a thin, "acceptable" body. At my heaviest, I used my weight as a buffer against pursuing any romantic relationships and hid myself in size 3x sweatshirts. It never occurred to me to think about all the good things I had to offer. I'm smart, I'm funny, I'm generous, I'm a caring and loyal friend, I READ, I'm a damn fine cook, and I do my best to never be boring. But, I could only focus on what I was lacking—a thin, toned body.

I've joined Weight Watchers at least five times in the past thirty years. Each time I lost weight—25 pounds, 40 pounds, and once, 85 pounds. And, within six months of reaching my "goal" (as determined by the WW charts), I had gained back all that weight with a few more pounds for good measure. I went through all the self-recriminations about being weak, unfocused, and too lazy to stick with the program. I was almost happy when I started taking a new medication whose main side effect was weight gain. Finally, I had a legitimate reason! I'd like to lose weight, but these damn meds!

I've been on both ends of the spectrum of reactions to my body. Crossing Boylston Street one lovely spring day, I had a well-coiffed, well-dressed man wearing $300 sunglasses scream at me: "Get out of the street you fat, f**king c**t!" Mind you, I had the light at the time.

And, I've had a very charming Greek taxi driver look in his rearview mirror at me as we drove through Central Park and say: "If you lived in my country you would be considered a Goddess!" He then invited me out to dinner, which I very reluctantly declined.

In the eye of the beholder, that's for sure.

About a year ago, I had a very interesting and heartfelt

conversation with my son. At the time, he was considering changing jobs; he had been offered a new position with an exciting company, Dia & Co. He would be the branding director of this innovative and quickly growing company that offered a subscription clothing service for plus size women. Because I fell into that category, we talked about what kind of advertising would appeal to larger women and more importantly, what kind of ads gave off negative vibes. We talked about how ridiculous it was that plus size women had so few choices for shopping and the ones they do have generally offered boring, matronly clothes that wouldn't make any size woman feel good. Dia & Co was starting an active conversation about women's bodies and what and who is beautiful, and offering many more choices for larger women. Fun, well-made, well-fitting clothes that make women feel confident and beautiful and empowered. I was, and am, so proud of Scott for wanting to be a part of changing the narrative about women's bodies and what beauty actually means. Let me just say now that this is not meant to be a commercial for Dia & Co. (although I do love them and am happy to spread the word). This is about how that conversation with my son on a Sunday afternoon, and then joining the subscription plan, helped me reach a totally different place about my body, my beauty, and my confidence.

Not so fun fact: Last year was the first year that a plus-size designer had a clothing line at New York Fashion Week. This year, there were more designers making beautiful clothes in large sizes and more plus-size models walking the runway. I'm talking about actual plus-size women—not the size 10 or 12 that some companies insist is plus-sized. There is not a universe where a size 12 is "plus size." Male fashion designers are speaking out about the inequity in the fashion world.

Personally, my decision to stop hiding in my clothes has

been life changing. I know that may sound silly—it's just some new clothes. But, I've been receiving pieces of clothing that, left to my own devices, I would never have tried on. This summer, for the first time in twenty years, I wore sleeveless tops. I bought a skirt...and wore it. I was sent the best fitting pair of jeans that I've had on my body since I was thirty-five. My closet has no boring, huge, clothes in it. They're all gone, never to be seen again. I open my closet and it's a happy place. There is nothing in there that I don't love, nothing that doesn't make me feel confident, pretty and happy when I put it on. I've got form fitting sweaters and silky, flowing kimono tops, and skinny jeans!

Skinny jeans!!! I'm actually wearing clothes that fit the body I have right now. And, I have come to realize that my body—although not what society would embrace as a beautiful body—is exactly that. A resilient, powerful, beautiful body. This body, in all its various sizes, has done amazing things. It has grown, nurtured and fed four beautiful babies; it worked three jobs at a time to support those babies; it's ridden horses and motorcycles—both at exhilarating speeds; it's carried protest signs and volunteered in women's shelters and cooked for the Democratic National Convention, Planned Parenthood, Joan Baez, and the homeless woman who lived outside my kitchen. This body has fought back relentlessly against multiple illnesses, injuries, and months and months of having toxic drugs infused into its veins. It's bounced back time after time after time and it's still bouncing back. My body has hiked and climbed down incredible waterfalls just to be able to sit and take in the beauty. It's given and received enormous amounts of pleasure. It's carried road kill to feed tigers and leopards and helped to socialize a herd of rescued miniature horses. It's baked hundreds of cupcakes and decorated dozens of birthday cakes and organized kick ass birthday parties for my kids. It's a good body. Not what it used to be, that's for sure. But, still ready to get up each day and live this life, which, sometimes is rough, but is also filled with joy and love and so many things that make me laugh every day.

Every body is beautiful. Every woman deserves to feel good about herself, deserves to look in a mirror and think, "I'm strong and fierce and beautiful."

Nobody should have to wait until they've lost 20 pounds to wear a cute dress. Or skinny jeans. Or mixed patterns. Wear whatever the hell you want. Wear what makes you feel pretty and powerful and HAPPY. Find your style; try on new things and rock everything you wear!

I love how my life has changed. To be just a few weeks away from sixty-nine years old and suddenly feel this good about myself, and my body, is pretty miraculous!

I thoroughly enjoy walking down the street, catching my reflection in a store window and having my first thought be:

"Damn! I look cute!"

Opinionated Mom, grandmother, chef, artist, foodie, reader and advocate for rights for all two- and four-legged beings. Lives in Vermont with two curmudgeonly cats and can't get by without books, Leonard Cohen songs, endless supplies of fresh fruit, British TV, art, flea markets and really good olives.

23 WHEN THE ELEPHANT IN THE ROOM IS YOU BY L.M. BENNETT

There is no way to sugarcoat this. When you lose a huge amount of weight in a very short period of time, your body simply cannot keep up. When you can only eat a banana-sized amount of food in one sitting and you do intensive training three to four times a week, your weight goes into free fall for the first year and a half. Mine did for sure; it was May 2016, and I had lost two hundred and forty pounds since the surgery.

I quickly learned the art of balancing body camouflage with thriftiness. I found cheap ways to tuck away saggy skin, wearing clothes that I could only keep for short periods of time while I rapidly dropped dress sizes. Denim jackets and boleros helped to hide bat wings hanging off of muscular biceps. Body-shapers held things together so I could wear body-hugging dresses without feeling too self-conscious. Outwardly, I had never looked better. I smiled more, I talked more, I projected confidence in a way I hadn't since I was four and told my Pre-K teacher I would not be going down for my nap. When those clothes came off, though, things were very, very different.

I watched in horror as breasts which were already small for

my size went from D- to B-cups. My high, round butt deflated. My waist was smaller, but the skin on my stomach looked like a Shar-Pei puppy's back. I had the face of a model, but my neck made me look old. My mouth grew parentheses. It was a total confidence killer.

The fear of disrobing in front of someone I liked and having them reject me for my body was very real, and very crippling. It's hard to feel sexy when you're constantly worried about the fleshy part of your upper arms spilling out of a short-sleeved dress.

It had a profound effect on my love life, and many times I allowed that fear to keep me from getting too close to people. I sometimes looked at online dating profiles and thought, he/she is too hot for me, and would never be interested in me. Sometimes when I was able to pull my head out of my ass, I ended up being pleasantly surprised.

At least short-term.

Sheila was the type of woman that, if my dad had come around to accepting my gayness, he would have actively tried to set me up with her. Driven, hard-working and smart, she was the kind of woman that my mom would have invited to a party just to introduce the two of us. The kind of woman they would call my "friend" with that little smirk that told me that they not only approved, but would like me to start planning grandchildren, ASAP. She worked in medicine and had musical chops. She was masculine-of-center, but preppy, manicured. Sheila preferred pressed jeans and velvet jackets and wore pantsuits at work. I thought she was cute in her pictures, and her cool, no-nonsense personality shone through in her profile. We struck up a conversation and quickly set up a date at a bar in the West Village.

One thing that people who have had gastric bypass surgery notice right away, even if we don't mention it, is other people's eating habits. We notice when you pick off the meat in your sandwich, when you choose to order the side salad instead of the fries, when you order kid-sized meals, when you declare yourself "stuffed" and send back a nearly full plate of food and request a to-go container.

We recognize our people, okay? So, when Sheila and I noticed each other discarding pizza crusts and taking forever to chew each bite, we looked at each other and started cracking up. We shared our stories of what led to getting the surgery, and the hilarious aftermath.

Do you know how refreshing it is to not have to explain why your fridge is overflowing with leftovers? Or, to make excuses over dinner, when you decide that whatever you order, it needs two plates? It's wonderful to have someone with a matching intolerance to cold who understands why you sometimes wear sweaters in the summer. I felt that I had found a kindred spirit in Sheila and was excited about the prospect of seeing her again.

We continued to see each other, and as a bisexual, it was so hard to find a lesbian who understood that even though you like boys and girls, you don't like them both at the same time. Some people like tuna fish and red Kool-Aid, but not together, you dig? I thought I had found a unicorn.

Then, the comments started. After a brunch with friends, they were trying to hail a cab and didn't have any luck, so Sheila put me to work. I was wearing a mustard-yellow skater dress that showed off my thick, toned legs, and we got one in no time flat. Later on, the driver admitted that he stopped because he thought I looked pretty, like Michelle Obama. We made conversation. Or, I made conversation, while Sheila watched me like a hawk.

Looking back, there had been red flags. The week before, while people watching at Union Square Park, we talked about celebrity crushes. I mentioned my heady love for Léa Seydoux, whether she was strutting around like a young Marlon Brando in *Blue is the Warmest Color*, or completely femmed up and glammed out like she was in *Spectre*. I stopped short of saying I would follow Chiwetel Ejiofor off a cliff. That prompted a comment from Sheila about having to watch me, because I was apparently attracted to everyone.

A short time later, I was having a birthday dinner with a colleague for a member of our team. Afterwards, Sheila accused me of being out on a date—with both of them.

Then there was the evening I brought lasagna pizza and wine to a friend who was stuck at home with her toddler on her birthday because she couldn't find a babysitter. For Sheila, that mission of mercy was a secret date—because I am that bold and prescient that when I plan to cheat on someone, I tell them about it in advance.

Friends, there were not enough hours in a day to have as much sex as Sheila thought I was having with other people. Bisexuals, stop me if you've heard that joke before.

I was not even comfortable enough in my body to randomly have sex with anyone, let alone half the population of Brooklyn. And frankly, I was sick of being called a low-key slut by the person I was dating.

The final pieces of the puzzle finally came together for me when she showed me an old picture of her with her band. She was in a short dress showing off all the goods, giving the camera a sultry look. Jiggity. I made the mistake of expressing a pervy sort of appreciation for it, adding quickly that I found it hot because it was her. She insisted that I thought it was hot because she was feminine, and in her old body. She questioned whether I found her hot the way she was now.

"I do," I said, thinking it was just that simple. It wasn't. I hit a raw nerve by accident. This is part of why dating women who are masculine-of-center can be very tricky; because unless they have that conversation with you, you really don't know how they feel about their bodies. Some (but not all) masculine-of-center women have mental, emotional or physical traumas that affect how they see their bodies, how they like to be touched and appreciated. Having more experience with women, I realize that now.

Sheila and I were simply not at the point in our relationship where we could have that frank a discussion about our bodies. It was too new.

Other than when I am playing dress-up with ties and pastel suits, I am a femme. I may love football and WWE more than any lesbian I have met, I may have wasted an entire year whipping around the streets of Liberty City in GTA IV, and be able to quote entire scenes from *Scarface* on a good day, but I am very much a girl. I love Sephora. Nothing makes me feel more fly on a summer day than a sundress and a French mani-pedi, with wild curls and sunglasses as big as my face. I can't even begin to unpack what it is like to be uncomfortable in your body because it is feminine in ways you hate, when you're still getting used to it being a new size. It's a double whammy.

Sheila and I ultimately folded for other reasons. Reasons that I, the queen of oversharing, feel discussing here would be super-invasive and tap-dancing over a fine line that shouldn't be crossed. Suffice it to say that she was going through something deeply personal. Either way, it was obvious that things were not going to work out.

I took three things away from my time with Sheila:

One, masculine-of-center women are also victim to the same insecurities that society imposes on feminine women. Actually, things are worse for them because they refuse to conform to what men find sexy and get ridiculed, harassed, intimidated or even sexually assaulted for daring to be themselves. Sheila internalized this somewhat; she found it difficult to believe that I thought she was sexy because she didn't believe she was.

Two, I had a type. Older, smart, funny, power lesbians were my jam, and I was probably done with men. This was great, because the type of woman I was ultimately looking for was starting to take shape in my mind, and I could more easily recognize and discard women who didn't meet my standards.

Three, I was still attracted to—and tolerant of—partners who were jealous and controlling. I was still willing to allow someone else to stretch out and make me uncomfortable just so they could occupy space in my life. My self-respect was the price I was willing to pay in order to keep the peace. This was not so good.

L.M. Bennett, 38, is a native of East Orange, N.J. and a surgical coder by day. She enjoys MMA, professional wrestling, roller derby, comic books, GBBO, classic rock and Jeff Goldblum.

24 HUSKY JEANS BY CATHERINE GENTRY

I was nine years old the first time it happened. My dad and I had gone to the mall with specific instructions from my mom to buy me a new pair of jeans. My heart leapt a little when I saw the display of designer jeans, some bedazzled, some with designer logos emblazoned on the back pocket. All the girls in fourth grade had them, and now I would too.

It was a disaster. Nothing fit. The harsh fluorescent lights of the fitting room did me no favors as I struggled to pull yet another pair of jeans over my hips. Sweating slightly from the exertion, I exhaled and pulled my stomach in as far as it would go, but they still wouldn't zip. Kicking the pile of discarded jeans already on the floor, I sat down on the small hard chair and cried.

I heard my dad's voice outside, asking if I was okay. I wasn't. But it hurt too much to say it. I emerged from the dressing room, trying to wipe away all evidence of my tears, the pile of jeans in my arms.

"They didn't fit."

"Not any of them?"

There was an uncomfortable pause as I shook my head, and my dad seemed unsure of what to do next. The saleslady hurried over, seeming to sense our discomfort. With a practiced smile, she looked me up and down, and pointed to a small area in the back. Her voice seemed especially loud.

"Sweetheart, let me have those. You need the Husky jeans."

"Husky" jeans. Even at nine, I knew what that term implied: fat. My head hung low, hoping nobody we knew saw us as we made our way to the rack tucked in the far recesses of the department and finally found one pair I could zip. They weren't cute, or fun, or fashionable like the regular jeans, but they fit.

It could've been a really awful day, one of those days that forever defines how you see yourself. But it wasn't. Instead of criticizing me or acting disappointed in my not-so-perfect body, my dad just hugged me. Then he told me I was beautiful. He still does, even after all this time, whether I'm in great shape, like when I got married, or striving to lose pregnancy weight after the birth of my third child. I think he just gets it, how it feels to be in a constant battle with weight and social expectations. He has struggled with his weight his entire life, and he always laughs and says that when he grows up, he will be tall and skinny. It hasn't happened yet.

I've often wondered what would have happened had my mom been with me on that shopping trip. I'm sure she would have been kind, but she has always been skinny, one of those rare girls whose mom encouraged her to eat more. She doesn't really understand. She doesn't know how it feels to be in a body that isn't what people deem acceptable.

Now that I have daughters of my own, I pay attention not to their size, but to their attitude. I want them to feel confident and powerful, not worry about thigh gaps and skinny jeans. It's a constant struggle, with the barrage of media images conveying impossible standards. Real bodies come in all shapes and sizes, and they need to know that if the jeans don't fit, it's not the end of the world. I want them to know they are unique and special and above all, loved for who they are. Mostly, I want to be like my dad, who tells me I'm beautiful, no matter what size jeans I wear.

Catherine Gentry is a writer living in Houston. Her work has been featured in The Houston Chronicle, The Princeton Alumni Weekly, Grown & Flown, Her View From Home, Literary Mama, *the* "Color:Story2019" *project, and on her blog,* Words Count.

25 LEGS: A SHORT STORY BY LIZ ESSE KAHRS

"You just can't wear fly front pants," my mother is saying, as we drive to Davidson's, a pre-teen clothing store in downtown Weybrook that specializes in half-sizes, which really means it has clothes for fat girls. At eleven, I'm tall for my age, five foot two inches, but my waist is wide and long, and my legs are short and chunky. When I look in the mirror, I see a thick tube, a container of fat. I want to be like Jean Marie McRae, small and petite, the cutest girl in my fifth grade class. Jean Marie has long, strawberry blonde hair. She wears it in ponytails tied with big furry elastics and sometimes even colorful ribbons. I would look ridiculous like this—my buckteeth spilling from my lips, my thighs rubbing against each other.

"Can I help you find anything?"

The man approaches us as we walk through the door.

"Yes. We're looking for my daughter."

He glares at me.

"The half-sizes are in the back."

As my mother charges through the store, I linger in the front, playing with the little tops and bottoms that look like doll clothes. I can see my mother picking through the racks, piling garments over her arm.

"Look at this cute peasant blouse! Oh, they have ponchos. Lily—you've got to see this smock top!"

She holds up the shirt for my inspection. It's brown and wide and there's a stretchy orange portion covering the chest; it looks like a pumpkin. She places the shirt over her arm and then reaches for a pair of flowered polyester stretch pants.

"And why don't you try these on? Just for kicks."

As my mother continues gathering clothing, I think about a pair of light purple Toughskins, the ones I want from Sears, the jeans everyone wears to school. But they are fly-front pants and would never fit me. Once, I tested my mother's theory by sneaking into the Gap to try on a pair of Levi's. I had to pick a larger size just to get them past my hips. The waist was so big, my butt crack showed through the opening in the back, and the denim cut into the tops of my legs.

Clutching the pile of tunics and jumpers, smock tops and polyester pants, oversized sweaters and dickies, my mother motions me toward the dressing room. If it hadn't been for Ruthie, I wouldn't be here. Ruthie's mother raving about "that new store in town for bigger girls."

Reluctantly, I accept the pile. In the dressing room, I shed my clothing, refusing to look in the mirror as I work my way into the brown smock top, the fabric tugging at my back. I pull on the polyester pants and feel the material adhere to my hips. Looking in the mirror, I see my thighs come alive—large bright blossoms stretched beyond their capacity. Whipping off the pants, I leave them in a ball on the floor.

"Anything fit?"

"I'm still trying things on."

I move my feet and rattle the hangers, pretending to try on the clothes. Staring at my legs in the mirror, I wonder why I got my father's legs instead of my mothers, why my legs look like tree trunks instead of long stretched out bowling pins.

"Any luck?"

"Nope, not yet."

I pick through the garments, searching for the least offensive items. Finally, I settle on a plain white peasant blouse and a pair of faded, elastic waist, bellbottom jeans.

The blouse fits, but the puffy sleeves dig into my arms. The jeans are okay and even a little loose. In the mirror, I turn, assessing myself from all angles. I look big, but not bad.

Pulling back the curtain, I stand before my mother.

"Finally, some clothes that flatter your figure!"

In the car on the way home, my mother lights a cigarette and cracks open the window.

"I'm so glad we found that place. I'm going back tomorrow to find more things for you to try on."

I cringe at the thought. Ever since my mother made me wear Chuck Taylor's with a dress to school, I have no confidence in her fashion sense.

"Maybe we could do it together," I say, "you know, like a mother/daughter thing."

"Oh, honey. Aren't you sweet?" She reaches for a licorice and pops it into her mouth. We pull into the driveway.

Inside, I head straight for my bedroom.

"Don't you want a snack?" My mother calls after me. "We have apples."

"Uh, no thanks." I'm already on the stairway. "I'm just gonna read."

In my room, I stand on my tiptoes and reach back into the closet to retrieve my box of Suzy Q's—but the box is empty. Sitting on my bed, I listen for noises through the heater vent, waiting for my mother to leave the kitchen to watch *The Guiding Light*. When I know she's gone, I sneak down the stairs to the kitchen, to the Lazy Susan, to the can of Betty Crocker chocolate frosting my mother bought the other day. I've been thinking about that can ever since—thinking about peeling back the metal tab and hearing that popping sound, thinking about unleashing all of that thick, chocolaty goodness.

On my bed, I stuff fingerfuls into my mouth. My goal is to finish the can, but I have to stop when my stomach begins to hurt. I lick my sticky fingers clean and try to use my tongue to remove the film from my teeth, but it is difficult—my tongue is swollen; it feels too big for my mouth.

I lie back on my bed and shut my eyes, my pupils darting back and forth beneath closed lids.

Liz Esse Kahrs novel, The Accidental Life of Daniel Sibley, *was a finalist in the novel-in-progress category of the 2018 William Faulkner Wisdom Writing Competition. You can find more of her work in* The Huffington Post, Amarillo Bay, Static Movement, The Boston Globe, *and* Shine.

PART 5

JUDGMENT DAY

RANDY SUSAN MEYERS

"It is not our differences that divide us. It is our inability to recognize, accept, and celebrate those differences."

—Audre Lorde

Vector Image by Ron and Joe

When I was a little girl, my best friend was Kathy Murphy. We lived on the same block and spent every waking moment (out of school) together, but we went to different schools—me, the local public school; her, the local Catholic school.

I was jealous of Kathy for many reasons: her freckles (oh, how I wanted them!) her brothers (oh, how I wanted protective brothers!) and that she didn't have to worry about what she wore to school each day—she had a uniform.

More than anything, I wanted to wear uniforms like Kathy. We had little money in our single-mother household—and what we had rarely went to clothes. Thus, the idea of reaching into one's closet and pulling out the right clothes every single day intoxicated me. I would, at long last, fit in.

But even more important than wearing the uniform was this: Kathy was Catholic. And, because she was Catholic, Kathy would go to heaven. I would not.

I knew this because Kathy told me in no uncertain terms that I could never, ever, no matter how good I acted, no matter how pure my thoughts, get into heaven. No Jews were allowed.

She did, however, mention something about Limbo—in which I pictured myself floating like a worm in a jar of water.

Religious training or customs were scarce in my house—until my mother re-married when I was thirteen, all we had was a small Passover Seder at my grandmother's home. Thus, during the years from age seven to twelve, I was an empty vessel ready to be filled by Kathy Murphy's declarations.

Being 'the other' is tough. For years, I worried about what eternity floating like a worm might feel like—and my concerns were nothing compared to the stories of the following women.

I pray that, during our lifetimes, Michelle Obama's words below soon become the words every one of us lives by:

"*Here in America, we don't let our differences tear us apart. Not here. Because we know that our greatness comes from when we appreciate each other's strengths, when we learn from each other, when we lean on each other, because in this country, it's never been each person for themselves. No, we're all in this together. We always have been.*"

—Michelle Obama

26 CONFESSIONAL BY STEPHANIE ENGLISH

WINNING ENTRY

I stopped believing in God when I was stick-thin, and have been tempted to reconsider since ballooning to twice my size. The God I hear about has an appetite for vengeance, and it seems He hungered for a chance to punish a skinny woman who loathed fat people by making her obese.

Growing up, I ate as much as I wanted of whatever I wanted, and I usually wanted sweets. Yet I was so skinny that a colleague wanted me followed into the bathroom after a dinner, convinced that the only way I could eat so much and be so thin was bulimia. My secret was not bulimia but good genes—which also gave me blonde hair, blue eyes, and good skin. I was "cute." Men looked at me; I was desired. I never imagined anything could change.

During those halcyon days atop my pretty perch, I was disgusted by fat people. I mentally threw stereotypes at them: Lazy. Pig. No willpower. Their bulges and excess flesh repulsed me, and that contempt drew God's attention to me like a dinner bell. He cast His eyes on me and saw a snooty little pop tart. He weighed me on His scales and found me wanting.

He threw a few pounds on me in my thirties—cleverly disguised as the leftovers of motherhood. As I tripped over my double chins on my way to forty, He ramped up the misery: a depressive episode during which I threw muffin after cupcake into the black hole threatening to swallow me from the inside. Within a few years, I'd gained so much weight that if I was a boa constrictor, it'd look like I'd ingested a middle school child. A foreign, moon-shaped face replaced mine in the mirror.

Waddling toward fifty and menopause (when weight gain is typical—ha!), I'm at my heaviest ever. Men do not look at me and I am not desired; I am invisible. The catcalls and wolf whistles echo in my past. I am the one greeted by others' labels: Lazy. Pig. No willpower. When I see a fat person, I know they're not happy. What's your story? I wonder. What's eating you up inside? Grief? Depression? Abuse? Loneliness? Far from my pretty perch, I know that no one plans to become fat or is happy about it. **Willpower is a fable that thin people tell.** As I cast my eyes away from someone's bulk, empathizing, I sometimes think that if I believed in God, He would be satisfied at the weight of my humility.

Stephanie English has thought of herself as a writer since she was 9 years old, yet only started writing in the past year. She has degrees in Magazine Journalism and English from Syracuse University and is a certified Editor in the Life Sciences. Stephanie lives with her family near Boston.

27 THIS IS MY BODY BY KRISTIN HILLS

WINNING ENTRY

This is my body.

My belly is soft and sticks out more than you think it's supposed to and I'm so glad I don't care about that anymore so glad I don't suck it in anymore when I see another person because I am wearing tight clothes that are comfortable for walking and you might look at me and see me red-faced and sweating and think What A Shame she's Let Herself Go she has to work so hard to move that big body what a shame she could be so pretty eh fuck you I am strong and beautiful and so is my belly my body and I would work hard no matter what size my body is because I like the feeling of the blood pounding in my ears.

This is my body.

This is the body I sometimes indulge with too much eating late at night and enjoying the feeling of being full too full because it is one of the only things that makes me sleepy this is the same body I take care of all day and fill with whole grains and plants and lots of water and if I want to eat expensive chocolate at night then I can and I will because I'm not going to regret things I didn't do enough later in my life EVER I'm going to savor whatever I decide to put into it I'm going to listen to IT and ignore your fucked up surface judgments so that I don't feel anxious about moving it slowly, slowly up the trail.

This is my body.

It can carry me places I don't have to go fast it can go slowly up hills and this is good I have two strong legs and a strong heart to pump blood to my muscles and if I go slowly I can still breathe up here going slowly I can see things I would miss if I were going fast this isn't a race I don't even have to race against myself fuck comparing fuck better than fuck how my body used to be how it will be it is just here and my neck has a nerve pinched and my brain wants to tear down the trail fleet-footed over the juts of granite and wood but my body is saying no and I listen because I love it my body.

This is my body.

This body is loved by more than just me my lover has adored my body for nearly a quarter century and he has watched it take up more and less space and he still loves my body because it is mine and it speaks to his it houses my soul my heart is his home and no matter how my body has changed he has desired it the same and not just for the soul it encases but for its own sake he may know my body better than I do he has loved it tenderly and fiercely and in dreams and in waking life and we have made three lives with our bodies together and he has watched my body swell with children and struggle to bring them out of it and he loved my body all the more for this our bodies were first to trust each other through emotion beyond emotion hip thigh breast belly face eyes eyes that see fingers that also see even shared breath that can see see all the beauty we have made together all the pain we have endured together our bodies speak in a way words cannot.

This is my body.

And even if he didn't love it anymore, I still would.
This is my body.

Posted 2nd August 2015 by motherlovebone

Kristin Hills lives and works between the redwoods and the sea in Northern California. Three of her short plays have been produced: #metoo, A Blanket for Benjamin, *and* Skirt Steak Surprise. *She dabbles in art of all kinds, while maintaining her day job as an administrator in early childhood education.*

28 RECORD OF WRONGS BY KIMBERLY ANN PRIEST

WINNING ENTRY

You get used to the mouth as a funnel,
loaded muzzle of a gun close range, cocked,
waiting to go off the moment you shove
a finger down your throat.

Bitch he says untired of counting every sin you commit
at 3AM when you peel your body out of bed
and tiptoe to the kitchen
for a sliver of chicken pressed onto a Wheat Thin,

because you've eaten almost nothing all day,
nothing you kept in your stomach,
the lean minutes that crawl the walls of this trailer
starved for some warm animal

to hug its floorboards praying *forgive us*
for we know not what we do.
If only the cupboards were not full of blanks
gaping with evidence that you have your mother's
    disease:

a bag of chips on her thighs, collapsing
one by one by one. You watched her and said
you'd never do this, be that way, the devils gloating
when they caught you descending the stairs, fifteen,

your father sizing you up, then saying to your mother
why can't you be skinny like this.
It's not that your husband means this too when he says
he is glad you are small because he is small

and—for his manhood—this is a very good thing.
And it isn't that he wants you to *feel bad*
about bulimia; it's just that he wants you to know
that he knows you do this.

Not like the cigarette he lights five miles from home,
smoking out the window of his car
so the scent won't settle in the seats,
then flinging it out into the darkness along the dirt road

while his headlights poke holes through the kitchen
where you wash dishes
aware that he will enter the back door smelling
of fresh cologne and nicotine;

but you won't say a word because this too
will be counted against you as keeping *a record of*
    wrongs—
no greater sin, he claims, forgiving you
completely—confiscating all your ammunition.

(previously published in *The 3288 Review*)

Kimberly is the author of White Goat
Black Sheep (FLP) *and her poetry has
appeared in several literary journals
including* The 3288 Review, riverSedge,
The West Texas Literary Review, Windhover, Ruminate Magazine *and* The
Berkeley Poetry Review. *She is a MFA
graduate of New England College, Assistant Professor at MSU,
reviewer for* NewPages, *and editor for the* Nimrod International
Journal.

29 ECHO BY LAUREN J. SHARKEY

WINNING ENTRY

It started small—having to catch my breath after going up the stairs, needing to recline my car seat back an inch...going up a size. "You might want to take some weight off," said my general practitioner during my annual, never once lifting his eyes from the clipboard.

I looked down and surmised it wasn't that serious. I mean, I could still see my feet. So, I did what everyone does: nothing. I mean, I told myself I would eat out less, exercise more, switch to diet soda. And I did all those things for about a week before going back to my routine of asking for extra bread at restaurants and late-night drives to Sonic.

It was a few weeks before I took my best friend out to dinner for her birthday. On the way home, I began to have that feeling, that "Oh my god I might need to pull over" kind of feeling. There was still a good amount of light outside, so I hit the gas, ran a couple of reds, and came to a screeching halt in my driveway before cursing myself for having so many keys. Finally through the door, I ran up the stairs to the bathroom and crash landed on the seat when I heard it.

The noise was loud and unforgiving. It echoed against the mirror, the tiles, the turquoise-tinted Mason jar bathroom set I'd bought off Etsy. I hoped the seat had simply slid off the bowl, and was in danger of disconnecting from the hinges, but I knew better. I lifted my bum and saw a crack in the white porcelain. I stared at the split for what seemed like a long while, wondering how my body was capable of fracturing something so strong and durable, and decided it was time to change.

I purchased portion control plates, bought a Ninja blender, and searched my room for the Fitbit I had long since cast away in lieu of charging the battery. But mostly, I wondered how it had gotten this far, how I'd let this happen.

All advice seemed to begin with the word "just." Just eat smaller portions, just cut carbs...just fix it. At the core of these helpful hints was a plea. A plea from friends and family to make myself familiar to them. I was no longer Lauren—I was Fat Lauren, Heavy Lauren, Have You *Seen* Lauren Lately?

As a plus-size woman, I am labeled as someone who doesn't care if they live or die, someone who is too lazy to "do anything about the problem," someone undesirable. I found myself before the mirror asking why this body was unacceptable? Why did this body need to be dominated, managed, erased? But I found no answers, no forgiveness—only the echo of the porcelain cracking, wondering if I could ever unite the halves of myself that had come apart.

Lauren J. Sharkey is a Korean American writer from Long Island, NY. Her debut novel, Inconvenient Daughter, *is inspired by her experience as an interracial adoptee. Her creative nonfiction has been published in* Dear Adoption, *Blind Faith Books'* I Am Strength *collection, and others. Learn more at* ljsharks.com.

30 DARK BODIES BY SHOMA WEBSTER

WINNING ENTRY

Skin as foreign as your native tongue
You don't belong here
Go back to where you came from
This place is for us
Not your kind

Your dark skin
Black skin
Ugly skin
Is not welcomed here

Find some other space to occupy space
Lift your mouth from the ground
Bite your tongue steadfast
You can't speak here
Better take flight because we don't sit with your kind
Dark as night
You dark skinned girl

Internalized words lead to a deep desire to peel off the
    layers of this dark skin
The hushed turned loud voices say, "how unfortunate
    to be born that way"
This is a crime and I'm the accused, cursed and
    punished with this dark skin
This ugly skin
That no one wants

Peel off the epidermal and dermal layer
Sure not to leave a trace
Left with flesh and bones
A carcass
Animals pick at the scraps to find a tortured soul

There are stories of other girls in faraway lands
Treated like filth because of their dark skin
There is no safe place
They're ashamed and in pain
Because the world has told them
Told us, to hate our skin
To hate our dark bodies

Their venomous words set out to poison us
Toxic to our souls, their words take hold
Invisible knife cut throat
Forcing us to loathe our bodies
The toxicity is overpowering and overbearing
Subconscious hate spews from the lips of the privileged
    and unprivileged
Those with dark skin alike, taking turns with the knife
Until there is nothing left
Dead women tell no tales

So, don't expect a quick happy ending to this woe
Like a package with a neat bow
The world has a long way to go
One step for woman
Equals zero steps for the dark woman
Feet trapped in quicksand
Left alone to contend
To heal
To fight
To exist in our dark skin

Shoma Webster is a student pursuing her clinical doctorate in Occupational Therapy. Recently, Shoma authored the piece, "Dark Bodies." In it, she draws from her lived experience as well as voices from others. In her spare time, Shoma can be found traveling and exploring different cultures from all over the world.

*O clement, O loving, O sweet Virgin Mary. Pray for us, O holy
Mother of God, that we may be made worthy of the promises of
Christ... Amen.*

I am ten. I am walking home with a friend from Girl Scouts.
We are walking through our neighborhood, up the last hill to
her house. She begins telling me something that horrifies me.
"When you turn eighteen," she says very solemnly, "they make
you go in for a special female exam." She goes on to explain (as
best she can with her limited ten-year-old knowledge) a Pap
smear. The horror of what she is saying to me slowly fills my
body from head to toe. It's a hot, uncomfortable fear that's so
sharp I can taste it. I try to think of ways I could get out of it.
"They make you do it," she explains. I go home, go straight to
my room and close the door. It never occurs to me to talk to
someone about it. Lumps of fear harden like rosary beads in my
throat. Good Catholic girls cross their legs when they sit—I
cross my legs so tightly that they almost meld together. How
could I ever open those legs up for someone to look inside? I

imagine a van full of men pulling up to my house on my eighteenth birthday to take me away for this exam. I decide then and there that I won't let them take me. I will run, I will scream, I will hide. I'm not going. They can't make me.

Growing up as a young Catholic female, I learned very quickly that my value lay in my purity and modesty. Role models for Catholic females are all virgins. The fact that the Mother of God is a virgin is so vital that it is part of her title. As a child, I prayed to "Virgin Mary," not even knowing what a virgin was. I thought it was part of her name. I innocently sang the lyrics to "Silent Night" every Christmas. *"All is calm, all is bright, Round Yon Virgin Mother and Child."* I had a picture book about St. Agnes, the patron saint of chastity and virgins. The picture book explained to me that young St. Agnes was forced to walk naked through the streets to a brothel. As she prayed, her hair miraculously grew longer and covered her naked body, preserving her innocence. She was then beheaded for refusing to lose her virginity. I vividly remember the description of the deep, red blood pouring out of her as she was beheaded. I had prayer cards with pictures of St. Maria Goretti, another virgin martyr. St. Maria is one of the youngest canonized saints, who was stabbed to death at age eleven for refusing to give in to the sexual advances of an older boy who worked on the farm with her. I learned she died screaming that she would not give in because it would be a sin.

It's difficult to wrap your brain around accepting your blossoming body when your mind has been filled with virgin martyrs. Why didn't God just save St. Agnes? All he did was make her hair grow long so she could keep her modesty while she was marched off to be executed. When I began menstruating, I didn't have anyone to talk to about it. I was poorly prepared. The only facts I knew came from the *Family Life* textbook my class read in sixth grade, and my well-read copy of

Are You There God? It's Me, Margaret. One weekend, I rode my bike to the public library and checked out two *very* dated books on menstruation. I wrapped them in a sweatshirt, hid them in my backpack, and rode home. I went in my room, closed the door, and devoured the books. I was hungry for information. I felt absolutely isolated.

I am fifteen. I am standing in the bathroom, crying. While blinking away hot tears, I stare at the tampon in my hand. Everyone I know uses tampons. No one ever told me they had trouble getting them in. Yet, here I stand, frowning at this monster in my hand. I read the directions. I read them again. I *still* can't figure it out. What I don't know is that I don't understand enough about my own anatomy to correctly use tampons. My Catholic upbringing doesn't allow for science or facts. My female parts are essentially a blur; something to be well-covered and not discussed. I never get that tampon in. I throw it in the bathroom trash and use only pads from then on. I never talk about it. What is there to say? I feel fear. I feel shame. I feel alone. The fear and disconnect from my own body gains momentum.

"To thee do we cry, poor banished children of Eve. To thee do we send up our sighs, mourning and weeping in this valley of tears."

I am seventeen. I can recite the words to "Hail Holy Queen" in my sleep. I have said this prayer over and over for years. I am not praying, as I had thought. I am reciting words that I do not comprehend. What does it actually mean to be one of the banished children of Eve? Well, I know that I carry Original Sin. I know that my body is a temptation to men, and I carry the responsibility to hide it under layers of clothing. I try to understand my changing body and my sexuality, but my very limited knowledge of sex is too intertwined with Catholicism and shame. The purpose of sex is procreation. Sex and sexuality in any other context are dirty and selfish, and my brain begins identifying any of these thoughts as such. I have no concept of how to embrace my sexuality, or my femininity, for that matter. I wear ill-fitting clothes, I feel ashamed of the body underneath those clothes, and I am utterly unaware of how to address these issues within myself. I spend the next fifteen years in this manner. I unknowingly force my physical body out of the essence of who I am becoming.

My eighteenth birthday arrives, and of course, no men come and force me to have a Pap smear as I had once feared. But, the fear that has been festering for years is only growing stronger as I start college. My reproductive system is covered by a heavy veil of mystery. My friends mention in passing about their annual exams. They laugh and say how awkward the exams are. I feel the rosary beads in my throat again. How are these people so comfortable with their bodies? Why am I so afraid of mine? I layer clothes over my curves. Is my skirt too short? Is my top too low? Oh, god. Cover it up. Cross your legs. Pray. As I enter my mid-twenties, I know that I can never find the courage to have that exam. No one ever asks, and I never talk about it. How can someone who can't even manage to use a tampon get through a visit with a gynecologist? I know as I get older that not getting a Pap smear could mean not detecting a deadly disease. I simply do not care. My fear of what I must go through to get a Pap smear is bigger than my fear of death.

I am thirty-three. I am at my first pelvic exam. I cry the entire time and am utterly humiliated. The provider who performs the exam is the first of three who will ask if I have been sexually assaulted, based solely on my behavior. I insist that I have not, although I am not convinced she believes me. I wonder, as I lie crying on that uncomfortable table, staring at the ceiling, why I can't just be normal. I don't want to be a banished child of Eve anymore. Maybe I never did. I don't want to see my body as a mysterious miracle of some far-off creator. I realize the only path to healing is to release myself from Religion. This is no easy task. Catholicism has her long fingers wrapped tightly around my cells, my womb, and my very being. Fingers like tree branches have long ago begun to grow out of that root ball of fear and shame in my stomach. Those fingers are moving along the rosary beads to the rhythm of the Hail Mary.

> *Hail Mary, Full of Grace*
> I breathe in, I breathe out
> *The Lord is with thee*
> I *need* to uproot that tree.
> *Blessed are you among Women*
> This woman *needs* to find her own way out
> *And Blessed is the fruit of thy womb, Jesus.*

Shame by B. Alexander

B. Alexander was well into her 30s before she even set foot on the path to Body Positivity. She believes strongly in women supporting women by sharing personal stories and experiences so no one ever feels as lost as she once did.

That's what the sign said, white and rectangular with bold red letters and gusting back and forth with the December winds.

PRIME SPACE.

What did that even mean?

From the comfort of her window seat at Yeast of Eden, her hometown coffee shop that Evangelina knew well but did not love, was incapable of loving, Evangelina watched the sign for a sign. Tuesday mornings were like that for her. With her hands, Evangelina hugged her white coffee mug, raised it to her lips, sipped, and set it down again. She liked the feel of the warm mug against her palms more than she liked the taste of bitter coffee in her mouth.

At the counter two seats to her right sat a young man, a college student by the looks of him, with his blue laplander hat pulled down tight over his ears and his human anatomy text spread out in front of him and opened to a spread-legged drawing of the female reproductive system and genitalia, all pink and flat and frightening. Evangelina had always hated those kinds of pictures, flat and vivid as they were with their

names for parts in bold print and thin black lines extending out
to almost but not quite touch them, leaving on the page a pause
of white, a gap between the line and the picture of the thing.
Clitoris. Vulva. Labia. Vagina. Evangelina couldn't help but
notice, and in noticing, a memory flared up of *Bailliere's Atlas
of Female Anatomy,* a thin blue volume bearing an armless
marble statue with soulless eyes on the cover. She had found
Bailliere's in her father's study when she was just a child, no
older than ten, and now remembered the feeling of heaviness as
her fingers had turned over the pages and found numbers that
corresponded with words for all the parts of her, pictures and
words for what was, she knew, her own body. Herself. *Uterus.
Fallopian Tubes. Egg.* Those words and pictures like impossible
alien worlds that existed beneath her own skin, that went
deeper even than the ropes of muscles all braided together,
sketched in fine pencil and colored pink on other pages. Evangelina remembered feeling that she should not know those
words but once known, could not unknow them, and feeling
that her mother would not, had she known, have allowed her to
sit spread-legged on the floor of her bedroom, looking in the
mirror at those corresponding parts of herself and saying their
names in a whisper, like she was studying for a test she would
surely never have to take. But Evangelina did look, and then
she knew what to call all the parts of herself, even the parts
deep inside, even though they were words in a language she
shouldn't know. What's more, because they were pictures in her
father's book, Evangelina knew they were words her father had
known about parts of her before she had even known them for
herself and that had made her feel...what? What had it made
her feel? Evangelina couldn't say exactly, because that was not
how her feelings worked, not, she thought, how feelings were
supposed to work. Feelings couldn't be labelled or defined like
the pictures in her father's book. All she knew was that the

book was a thing to be put back on its shelf exactly as it had been before she had even entered her father's study, and so she did. Not that that could undo her knowing, scrub her mind of those pictures and words the way her mother on her hands and knees scrubbed the green linoleum kitchen floor, wanting it to look as new as it had the day it was laid down. No. Not like that.

She was staring. Evangelina hadn't meant to stare, but the young student in the laplander hat who sat with his right hand on his chin and his left hand raised with a yellow highlighter, glanced at her now, smiled, and she moved her eyes to a loose thread on her burgundy sweater. She gave the thread a quick tug, but it didn't break, only began an unraveling. What did it matter? Christmas was already over, so why should she care? Still, she felt that it did. She smoothed down the thread and looked out of the window to PRIME SPACE, the sign subject to each gust of wind, large or small.

Evangelina knew she looked suspicious, guessed that the student could read her mind. She could not look at him but raised her mug and took a sip so casually she knew she couldn't possibly have looked casual. The wind only seemed to blow one direction today, as maybe it always did, but that sign, PRIME SPACE was constantly being pushed away from her, in the direction of the cars traveling along the street, in the direction that took them out of town. A westerly direction? An easterly one? She didn't know. Maybe it was north, even. Or south. Evangelina never could tell about those larger directions in the world, the ones a compass could have told her had she had a compass, had she cared. And she did, really, sort of care right now which she found odd because usually she didn't. Usually she wasn't bothered about not knowing her place in the world and which direction she was headed, but just now for whatever reason she wanted to know in which direction the wind was blowing, which way it was pushing the PRIME SPACE sign. Russell would have cared about such things, she knew. Her husband always cared about such things. And he would have already figured out the direction, because he just naturally knew without even needing a compass.

Evangelina lifted again the white mug to her lips, the coffee now cooler than the surrounding air, and while this was something she minded, she felt no pressure to go to the trouble of standing and walking around the man with the laplander hat and the anatomy book and over to the counter against the yellow wall where six varieties of coffee waited, any one of which could have warmed her up, but only one of which—the decaf house blend—she could have chosen for herself.

Evangelina had looked outside and she had looked at the student, but now for the first time Evangelina lifted her eyes, just a little, to notice an oversize peppermint candy the size of a medium pizza wrapped in clear plastic and hanging from a red ribbon that reached up to a row of little blue light pinecones planted in fake pine garland. They were pretty, Evangelina thought. They were the sort of decorations she might look for at Kohl's for 50% off the day after Christmas, the sort she might even be lucky enough to find, though not enough of them to stretch across her front room window, not with all the shoppers she would be elbowing against. Still, these lights would be something to look for. There was also sparkly red beaded garland, like Mardi Gras beads but more dignified, looped at uneven intervals—some three inches, some five, and so on— throughout the fake greenery. That added a nice splash of color and looked good with the peppermints and occasional red bulbs. Yes, that would be nice.

Evangelina's neck began to hurt. That was the way bodies worked after a while when one part would do something for just a little too long. She grew aware of a slight pull in the back of her neck, and a small cramp in her lower back. Slowly, painfully so, she bent her head down until her chin touched her chest, then turned her head to the right only to see the student again, not studying now, his cheek smack-dab against the over-sized vagina, asleep. Had he no shame? No shame whatsoever? The sight made Evangelina terribly uncomfortable, even if her primary view was the back of his laplander hat which was bright blue and had a door on it that looked like an old phone booth, or something very much like it. She had known from the moment she saw it that the hat was a cultural reference to a television show that was not a part of her culture, but that was all she knew, and she hated feeling left out of a secret.

Evangelina wanted to go and shake him awake, or at least slide the book out from under his face and close it. Books could become pillows to tired students. Even she knew that. But the least he could have done was close it first.

Dawn Burns received her MFA in fiction from the University of Notre Dame and teaches writing at colleges in Indiana. Her story "Evangelina Contemplates 'Prime Space'" is a chapter from her thematic novel Evangelina Everyday. *Dawn can be found online at dawnburns42.com, and in person by Lake Wawasee in Syracuse.*

33 INFLUENCES BY ELIZABETH SINCLAIR CADY

Where do I begin to discuss the relationship I have had with my appearance? I am fifty-one years old, five foot five, 134 pounds, and attractive, and I have never liked my body more than I do now.

I have never been thin enough, firm enough, or tall enough, and yet how well I have endured through several health scares and my weepy entry into our empty nest. My body has earned my respect and I try to keep its needs (exercise, diet, mindfulness) in the forefront—not an easy task given my history of feeling it was always subpar.

And I'm not sure why I've come to terms with my body. I think losing so many friends and family this past year helped. But perhaps it has more to do with gaining wisdom as I've aged. I am grateful to still be alive. Looking through dozens of family photos recently, I thought of the ways in which my two grandmothers influenced my body image.

My earliest memories include my beautiful Italian grandmother, Carlotta, who was almost always smiling. There is only one time I can recall when she was angry and her face was not radiant with light—my grandfather (my prince then and now) had upset her and she was frowning and telling him to be quiet, that she was taking care of whatever it was, and he should let it be. And I think he listened and perhaps understood, as we all listened and appeared to understand that Carlotta had whatever it was under control. Other than that one instance, my grandmother is smiling in my thoughts, cooking or picking berries with us at camp or in her garden, or visiting with family and friends—always happy and full of life. I felt empowered in her presence, and my appearance was never in question.

Carlotta was not thin, firm, or tall, yet she still exuded the kind of self-confidence that I could only dream about.

My other grandmother, Jeanne, a Scottish widow, was less enchanting to me and yet no less radiant in her own right. She was competent and commanding in both the yard and the kitchen, and perhaps as beautiful in her blonde hair and blue eyes as Carlotta was with her dark eyes and black hair. And Jeanne was funny and always on the go. But she made me repeatedly question my appearance and demeanor through her unsolicited opinions: "Why do you wear your hair like that?" "Have you gained weight?" "Why are you always reading?" "You need to wear more makeup." "You know, your sister is the one men will want to sleep with, but they'll want to marry you." (Consider suggesting that to a sixteen-year-old girl, much less your granddaughter.) And if it was not a comment, it was a well-timed, raised eyebrow.

Jeanne was not thin, firm, or very tall either, but she had so much self-confidence. Yet she would undergo three facelifts— the first while in her forties.

My mother was ever present too, and lovely—also not thin, firm, or tall—but she was gently supportive and held less sway on my developing self-image than Carlotta and Jeanne.

We absorb the good but the less good sinks deeper. It resonates and haunts us. Thin is better and fat is just wrong. Appearance matters and being attractive means you matter more, or so my sisters and I were led to believe, thanks, in part, to Jeanne.

I could tell you about my grandfather, Frank, who would later reside with us after Carlotta passed away, providing the emotional support my sisters and I lacked through high school and college, given my father's extramarital affair and my parents' divorce. Frank provided unconditional love and any talk about our appearances would have been poorly received—his granddaughters were wonderful in every way.

I could tell you about my father's comments regarding female appearance (including weight, hair length, and chest size) over the years. How they mattered. How they weighed upon me and the rest of my family.

My sisters and I were blessed to grow up in a loving environment, but the repeated emphasis on appearance would take a toll on us—especially with society confirming this in so many ways.

If middle age has brought me nothing else, it has granted me the wisdom and peace to truly appreciate my body, and perhaps understand that everyone who played a role in my development was also young once. And they had their own influences.

Elizabeth Sinclair Cady lives in the heart of New York with her husband and Zelda the wonder dog. She loves her family, championing women, and her thighs.

34 SHORT STORY FROM A POST-DIVORCE MEMOIR: PARTNERS AND OTHER CONUNDRUMS BY NELL CARROLL

Aaron was "Yurt Boy" to my friends because he was younger and, well, lived in the yurt. After our initial romp in the yurt, we continued to trade sexy texts and a couple phone calls. I discovered he couldn't spell, and it sometimes took me a few minutes to understand what he was trying to communicate. He didn't give a shit about autocorrect. But he didn't mind that I was carrying extra weight and he was strong enough to treat me like I was a waif. I wasn't sure when I could see him again because my son was back home. I was still reeling from the yurt escape and somehow it didn't seem real, more like a scene from a romance novel.

He was a fling, though, and I needed to settle down and look for the real deal. At the urging of friends, I signed up for eHarmony and was going to try online dating. I chose that one because it gave you a free month, and, based on all the questions people had to answer, I thought maybe there was a chance for me. OK, I was also brainwashed by the adorable couples in love on the commercials. They weren't perfect looking so maybe...

I labored over those questions. I wasn't even sure what I wanted or who I was after my divorce. How could I answer these honestly? There had to be someone out there for me. I found a cute photo that I didn't have to Photoshop too much. The danger of being a photographer is that you have skills to misrepresent or enhance your natural beauty. I sent in the profile and waited, not patiently.

Now, the reason I hated online dating was that you're being judged by your looks. My own choices were based on looks. For God's sake, smile if you want me to like you. Oops, too skinny for me. That is a strange looking shirt. Why, oh why, did you take that selfie in the bathroom? Who are all those women in the photo with you?

I was sure I was being judged the same way and, ironically, it pissed me off. Give me a chance, I thought. No, I am not a five foot eight blonde with a perfect Pilates body, which seemed to be the Texas standard. Sometimes 100-percent real, full of energy and funny is a hard sell online. I hated myself for not treating the matches the way I wanted to be treated.

Then there was the etiquette. Who was supposed to reach out first? Did I sit and wait? That wasn't really my style, but when I did try to make a connection, all I heard were crickets, no one home. I thought maybe I should just ignore it for a few days. I was obsessed, not even waiting until my son had gone to bed to check matches. That wasn't who I wanted to be, waiting to see who chose me, and who thought I was worth meeting. There wasn't a flood of activity like friends told me would happen. I guess being over forty and having a child wasn't really what men my age were looking for. In fact, it appeared to me that men my age wanted women who were ten to fifteen years younger, who could still have children. Men ten years older were not interested in me, likely because they were empty nesters and wanted to have a partner with the freedom to do things at a moment's notice.

Finally, a nice one came through, a kind of handsome, guitar-playing, cowboy-boot-wearing guy. We chatted online about where we grew up, and our love for the outdoors and music. In reality, he made more sense for me than Aaron did. Eric was my age and had a grown-up son. He had been divorced for a few years. From a small town in west Texas, he enlisted in the Army and traveled the world, ending up in Germany, where he met his ex-wife. They had moved back to the U.S. after his stint in the Army. That was all he told me about her during our "get to know you online chats." Soon, we graduated to phone calls and texts. He was funny and understood my sense of humor. He called me by my given name, Wynelle, rather than my more common nickname. He said it was different and pretty. However, Eric and I soon discovered we might have a conflict when we began to discuss what we did for a living. I was pretty open about being a journalist, but he had been cagey. I was beginning to get suspicious and finally asked him point blank.

"What do you actually do to make money? It seems like you have been off work a bunch lately. Does that mean you're unemployed?"

"Well I have been avoiding this question because you are the enemy."

"Pardon me?" We had not even met yet. How could I be his enemy?

"I am a cop. We are not supposed to trust or deal with journalists. And to date one…" his voice trailed off.

Ah, that made sense, I thought. I was well aware of the tension between police and the media.

"Personally, I've always thought that cops and journalists

should date. We have the same dark sense of humor and often face stressful situations in our lives."

"We'll see. I know I like you though, and I just won't tell you anything work related that you might want to report on."

"Deal."

We needed to figure out when to meet in person and this scared me to death.

Nell Carroll lives on a hobby farm near Austin with her son, dogs, cats, horses, donkey, chickens and ducks. She spends her spare time on the fifth draft of her novel. Her interest in writing led her to participation in adult storytelling.

I signed up for Weight Watchers the first time at twelve years old. It was the mid-eighties, and I can vaguely remember someone saying I was the youngest member to join. Even if that were the case, it wasn't an award I wanted.[1] Starting Weight Watchers was supposed to be my tool. A way to escape the prison I'd put myself in. No one coerced me into joining. My mom, grandmother and I rallied as a team to get healthy in a medically approved way. I did well in the beginning. I even enjoyed it. At some point, for reasons lost on me now, we stopped going to those meetings. I found the weight I'd lost.

I asked my mom recently if she remembered a time when I wasn't overweight. She thought for a moment before replying, "Maybe when you were really little?"

Our family has joked that I was born already addicted to sugar. During her pregnancy, my mom craved most all sugary delights. She especially loved presweetened cereal with a hearty scoop of granulated sugar. When I was born, a couple of weeks past the due date, I weighed eight pounds twelve ounces. My mom gained about forty pounds during the pregnancy on her four foot eleven frame; however, she left the hospital only fifteen pounds from her pre-pregnancy weight. She had been merely the vessel for my parasitic life force.

Once I started elementary school, I was already comparing myself to the other girls. While they were playing with dolls, putting puzzles together, or running around the playground at recess, I was wondering why I looked so different. My belly pooched out. My hair was stick-straight and brown. My eyes were light, but boring. I didn't have nice smooth skin with an even skin tone; I was mottled with freckles.

I headed into puberty very early, which seemed to amplify my weight and insecurities. By fourth grade, I'd stopped growing. All the girls I envied were getting taller and more beautiful, with their lean bodies and smooth skin. Once one of the tallest girls in my class, I had flipped overnight to the extra-pudgy short girl splattered with acne.

A constant battle raged in my head. I'd finally learned that portions played an integral role in my weight issues. Something seemed to be disconnected. I was always hungry. While I ate, I'd be thinking and looking forward to whatever meal or snack came next. I liked washing the dishes, preferably alone, because then I could sneak extra bites of mashed potatoes or pilfer cookies from the bottom drawer of the fridge. All the while, I hated my body.

I attempted the role of the happy-go-lucky girl next door. I tried out for the cheer squad. Auditioned for plays. I was nice to everyone and didn't play into the clique system. Irony is being the largest person in the room, yet invisible. The loneliness intensified the cravings. Sitting in the shadows, I used food to numb the things I didn't want to feel.

Thanks to the hairstyle trends of the late '80s and early '90s, I'd come to accept my hair. There was nothing I couldn't accomplish with a perm and a can of White Rain. My eye color had changed into a green/brown hazel and became my best feature, if only in my own mind. My mom taught me how to use makeup to play up my eyes. However, the hairspray and eyeshadow created a false sense of security and didn't address the heart of my issues.

After a series of questionable choices the summer before my senior year, I found myself pregnant. Prior to the pregnancy, I'd lost a lot of weight and finally felt comfortable in my body. Even as I regained the weight, I didn't worry about how I looked. I was on the verge of becoming a teen mom, but I was happy. I wasn't overweight—just pregnant. All short girls look bigger when pregnant. About six months into my pregnancy, I ran into a former classmate. "Wow. You got FAT," she exclaimed.

"No, just pregnant," I told her.

As quickly as I had shed it, I dove headfirst back into the suit of shame.

Twenty-six years and two more kids later, I despise my body. My husband calls me "cute," but never "beautiful." On more than one night, I've laid in bed with tears staining my pillowcase. "If I could just be thin, everything would be so much better!" Like I could just wake up skinny. A modern-day fairy tale if I ever heard one. Skinny would increase my bank account. Make me more successful at work. Clean and redecorate my house. I'd finally finish that novel. My skin would be flawless, my hair sleek and manageable. Every woman is beautiful and successful in her own right, but I won't have any of that until I'm thin.

Somehow, I've based my happiness on an arbitrary number on the bathroom scale or the size of my jeans. In search of nirvana, I've tried many diet plans, most of them more than once. Weight Watchers reigns number one in attempts.

My logical side tells me multiple times a day to either

accept my body as is or do something about it. I'm determined, until the hunger sets in. While scrolling Instagram, admiring women of all shapes and sizes, wholly comfortable in the temples they have designed, I crave the feeling I assume I'd feel from shopping in the petites section.

I fear I'll always look at my body with disdain even if I can overcome my self-deprecating behavior. Even if I am able to achieve what I believe to be a healthy size for my five-foot frame, it won't be enough. I fear I will only be able to focus on the flaws underneath my clothes, like sagging skin and non-pregnancy-related stretch marks. I fear I will not develop a healthy relationship with food. At the core, perhaps my lack of positive body image is really a lack of a positive Heather image.

A few years ago, someone said to me, "I'd be happy if I could be your size." Those nine words still haunt me. My body is not, and likely never will be, one to envy.

Heather Clift is an award-winning writer with a passion for all things Southern. Her short stories have been published in a variety of anthologies and magazines. In her spare time, Heather enjoys binging on Netflix, making to-do lists, and grammatically correcting memes. She is currently working on her first novel.

36 SO, I'M FAT. I'M TOTALLY OK WITH THAT BUT YOU MIGHT NOT BE BY FRANCES DANGER

I've always been a big girl. I'm pretty solidly built anyway, but I'll be the first to admit my fluffiness stems more from my love of all things food rather than genetics or having "big bones."

When I was a toddler, I won a nationwide "Beautiful Baby" contest sponsored by a major department store. Dressed to the nines in a Western shirt and overalls, I played pretend patty cake and smiled up a storm as the photographer shot away. The result is one of my favorite pictures of myself, a child unblemished by the weight standards that would dog her throughout the rest of her life. I was big even then, but I still won that contest and was officially certified as beautiful. If only that same standard of beauty applied to grown up me.

Instead, I was relegated to being "pretty," or, more to the point, I'd be so much prettier if I just lost some weight. Gee, thanks?

I learned very early on that if I was going to have any self-esteem at all, I'd have to refuse to accept these backhanded compliments. Sure, I was pretty, but I'd be better, prettier, more beautiful if I wasn't so fat. That's bullshit.

The thing is, though, I am beautiful. I've got great skin, a lovely smile, and my hair is better than yours. My weight contributes to that beauty in that I have never tried to be what everyone else told me I should be, and it freed me to accept myself as I am. If there was ever a gift wrapped in an insult, that was it. It's why I can say I'm fat without denigrating myself, and that's awesome.

Recently, I was at a fairly busy event and was trying to leave early. It was very cramped, so I chose the path of least resistance: the ramp. There was a group of people firmly planted on the ramp as I made my way down. "Make way," I called. "Fat girl coming through."

As if in slow motion, one of the men turned his head towards me, flipping his hipster dreads to one side, and fixed a discerning eye on me, focusing (after giving my body a once over) on my face. His eyes lit up with concern.

He reached for me as I passed and said, "Don't say that, honey! You're beautiful." He smiled, pleased with himself that he'd overcome some sort of social litmus test by seeing the "real" me.

I stopped and stared at him, his smile more like a laser-focused dagger than the self-congratulatory enlightened one I'm certain he thought it was.

"I never said I wasn't beautiful," I responded. "I said I was fat. You're the one who thinks the two are mutually exclusive, otherwise you wouldn't have equated the lack of one with the other. It sounds to me like you have way more of a problem with me being fat than I do." I watched as his smile faded and I continued on my way.

And that's life as a fat girl. Even your compliments can be putdowns. It's so ingrained that people don't even notice they do it.

It happened again the other night. The person I was riding

with apologized for how cramped the backseat I'd be seated in was. "It's okay. I'm fat. I'm used to it."

"You're not fat. You're pretty."

No, fucker, I'M BOTH. I do not have to be one or the other. I almost prefer those who are in my face about it. Call me a fat bitch all day long. At least you're being honest with both of us.

Those that think they're above it, telling me I'm beautiful, lying about my weight ("You're not fat!"), full of good intentions and political correctness, they bother me the most because they don't even recognize how condescending they are being. With that behavior alone, they contribute more towards perpetuating the societal acceptance that being overweight makes you flawed, not entitled to feeling good about yourself, or somehow less than those who are a size 2. Just because you smile when you say it doesn't make it palatable or legitimate.

So yes, I'm fat. I'm also beautiful (I have a certificate that says so). I can be both at once (I'm excellent at multitasking) and I don't need society's input on the matter to make it true. When it's my time to go, I'll go knowing I lived my life to the fullest, in more ways than one.

Frances Danger is a proud Mvskoke Creek/Seminole. She writes on issues of racism, cultural appropriation, Indigenous rights, and personal experience pieces that have been published in local, national, and internationally known web properties. She prefers Mal over Han, has more eyeshadow than you probably, and is definitely, 100% #notyourmascot.

37 SIZE ZERO? ZERO SENSE BY KATYA DUFT

A friend of mine was recently interviewed on TV for a show about karate. She was in her element, working out and teaching martial arts at a gym she manages. Afterwards, the show was posted on YouTube and viewers could offer comments. Sadly, I realized that despite my friend's obvious display of talent and athleticism, the one thing people chose to comment on was her large frame.

That hit close to home for me. Never having been skinny, I have nevertheless always been athletic. Starting with volleyball at seven, then skiing at ten, I continued to take part in all school athletic activities from then on. These days, I run regularly and go on long hikes. I have also participated in stair climbing charity competitions for the last ten years, where I get to climb up skyscrapers, the tallest probably being the seventy-three-floor US Bank building in downtown Los Angeles!

At the age of twenty-four, while still living in Russia, I took a training course to become an aerobics instructor. I passed all the tests (both theoretical and practical ones) but couldn't get certified due to being "bigger than a regular instructor," in the words of the course creator. I lacked a bit of flexibility, but not strength or knowledge, and promised to work on it if they passed me, but the jury refused to, because I didn't "visually fit the image." That was quite a blow to my confidence, and I have never aspired to be an instructor again.

About the same time, I became a fan of belly dancing and started taking classes that I enormously enjoyed. By the time I moved to LA, I had been doing it for several years, so when I saw a Craigslist ad about joining a belly dancing performance group, I didn't hesitate to apply.

At the audition, all the applicants were taught a dance routine that I had no problem recreating. The organizers picked me, along with several other women and took us to a different room. That seemed like a good sign, and I couldn't help getting excited. The group leader praised me on my moves, but then confessed that the performers only wear size zero costumes, so another curvy woman and I wouldn't be able to join the group, despite our experience.

The other woman and I stared at each other for a moment and then burst out laughing. That sounded like nonsense, because most belly dancers have at least a bit of a belly, generous breasts, and sizable hips. "Sorry, but this is LA style belly dancing!" announced the group leader. How can you argue with that?

So often in life, we let stereotypes win and don't consider anything outside of what we see with our eyes. Having extra weight and being athletic are not necessarily mutually exclusive. I work out and have annual physicals to make sure my blood tests and other vitals are within healthy limits. I watch what I eat and always try to improve myself. What you see is not always what you get.

Katya Duft is a public transit blogger (Tales from the Bus) *and a recent Moth Story Slam winner; frequent participant of storytelling shows and contests in Los Angeles. She is also a linguist fluent in English, Russian, and French, who works in post-production.*

My body. So many things have been said about my body. I wish I could say it started when I was an adult, but it didn't. At thirteen, I got my period and everything changed. I was so angry, because I was not ready to grow up. Now I had to deal with the real possibility of getting pregnant. In the same year, my weight moved to other places. Suddenly, my teen bra was not doing the job. While I was trying to process this as practically a child, my friends no longer wanted to be around me. Now they made fun of me and called me "fat" and "big butt." I didn't understand what I did wrong. During that time, I observed that I had a lot of unwanted male attention. I had my childhood Hollywood crushes, but I was not ready to date.

I eventually lost the baby weight. In high school, the women around me: friends, family, and classmates, encouraged me to spend a lot of time on makeup and hair, even though the few boyfriends I had didn't seem to care about either one. My friends still made fun of me at school, even though I was no longer fat. In middle school, I was afraid to say much. When I got to high school, I angrily railed against their insults when they made fun of me. Then I would go home crying. I was so oblivious. Those little girls were probably just jealous. It was so sad, because even though I was a very nice person, they made fun of me.

My dad died when I was sixteen. He was sick for a whole year. My close friends were supportive during that time, but most of my classmates did not ask any questions. After he died, one classmate that had made fun of me for a long time asked me how I was doing. It made me angry that I spent a year knowing my Dad was dying, but it wasn't real to anyone else until he was dead. I didn't believe she was genuinely trying to be nice. I told her she could go fuck herself. I couldn't wait to graduate high school. I thought people would change their attitudes and assumptions as they matured and became adults.

After working a few jobs in my adulthood, I found that those little girls never did grow up. They were everywhere: your mom, your sister, your friend, your coworker. When I was a kid, they used to call me Carrot Top and chubby, and now the insults were more passive aggressive.

I like to wear V-neck shirts. A supervisor invited my husband and me to dinner with her family. I wore a V-neck T-shirt and a sweater to her house. The next day she said to me, "Do you watch Food Network?" and I said, "Yeah." She said, "Do you watch Paula Dean?" I said, "Sometimes." She said, "I like Paula Dean, but I hate how she wears V-neck shirts," while looking me right in the eye. I never went back to her house, and I haven't seen her since.

You can't always get away from them. As I said, I like to wear V-neck shirts. I also like to wear scoop neck shirts. While my shoulders are wide, lots of times the sleeves slide down. A few very conservative family members felt the need to tell me that they hated when women showed their bra straps. For a couple of years, I wore sweaters on top of my T-shirts, even in the summertime.

In my mid-twenties, I was still listening to those little girls. The women in my family raised me to believe that men were the ones who were hard on women and had ridiculous expectations. At that time, I was taking a psychology and a sociology class. I was shocked to learn that women were often the ones tearing each other apart. The stereotypes about clothes and hair and makeup did come not from men. They were perpetuated by other women! My family raised me just like most girls; I was supposed to fit into some ridiculous box which fits no one.

I moved to D.C. and went to film school for a while. Animating was labor intensive, and I did not have time to fix my hair and makeup. All I could think of was that my mom and my sister would be so ashamed of me, and I still let those little girls get to me.

The last straw was the haircut. When I moved to D.C., I had shoulder-length hair. I wanted to donate my hair to Wigs for Kids. I let my hair grow out for three years. I always wanted to get a pixie cut. No one believed I would do it. When it was long enough, I got that pixie cut! But I didn't get the response I expected. No one cared that I donated my hair. In fact, the only thing women cared about was my haircut. Several different women called me "brave." Several women my age said, "I could never cut my hair!"

I wasted twenty-one years listening to those little girls. Fat people called me skinny and skinny people called me fat. The truth is, I will never make them happy. So I won't apologize. I am a voluptuous, medium person, and I am still rocking that pixie cut.

I was born and raised in central Pennsylvania. I served four years in the Air Force. I met my husband at my first duty station, and he is still serving in the Air Force. We are currently living in Kansas, where I am studying accounting.

39 WE NEED MORE RUBENS BY DEDRIA HUMPHRIES

I grew up thin as a rail, which was an inoculation against self-hatred, but I was always aware that my older sister was fat. She wasn't; she was big and tall, nearly six feet tall in an era when tall women were not valued. Petite women were considered ideal, and being tall ate at a woman's self-worth. As a result, my sister grew into a woman with self-defeating behaviors and ultimately became obese. Now she is so heavy that she can only drag her body around, and I fear she may end up in a wheelchair.

While the main theme of *Waisted* does not reflect my personal story, I can relate, because the idea that a heavy woman needs to be fixed has influenced a woman I so love. The focus on a woman's weight, to the exclusion of her other personal features, is damaging to her self-esteem. In fact, such intense concentration sabotages her efforts to be at a healthy weight. For a woman to feel that what she eats determines her whole life creates a great deal of anxiety. It seems food not only causes big problems, but solves them as well. Food becomes everything.

As a community college professor of writing, I read many essays about this issue, about how a person should not be judged by her appearance, and yet that theme has an air of futility because everyone knows women are judged that way. The American dream of a career and a family has historically balanced on the scale of appearance, and nothing is more important than a woman's size. What a burden for young women to carry, along with all the other crap American culture heaps on us. What we need in the modern world is acceptance of women like those painted by Rubens.

Dedria A. Humphries Barker is the author of Mother of Orphans: The True and Curious Story of Irish Alice, a Colored Man's Widow. *Her work has appeared in* Salon.com, *and* Redbook *magazines, and published by the Michigan and Ohio historical societies, and the Society for the Study of Midwestern Literature. The Detroit native lives in Lansing.*

40 ON BEING PROPER BY E. B. MOORE

A siren wailed. I pulled right, ready for the police to pass, but the car bore down behind me as I applied the brakes, rear then front, stopped, and kicking the kickstand down, leaned my bike by the side of the road. I stood on the gravel verge, blue lights blipping as I waited and wondered why they sat there gesticulating at one another.

Finally, two troopers in black boots eased out of their car. Clones in dark glasses under flat brimmed hats, they stopped their whispered argument as they closed the distance between us and settled heavy gun belts low on their hips. Each man rested a hand on the butt of his pistol. Was I dangerous?

Maybe so at six feet tall, a little taller with the helmet, but two of them with guns against one of me, and me a girl at that. How could that be daunting?

"...the hair," I heard one say. He adjusted himself, shook one leg, and straightened the flair of his jodhpur-like pants. They stood before me, bow-legged, heads tilted, peering. At my hair?

Had Mother been right all along? Long hair means trouble. But surely not an arrestable offense.

At first (mid-1940s, I was six), she doubted my hair would grow beyond my earlobes. It never had before, so why would I think otherwise. She only trimmed the shaggy edge with her scissors. Appearance mattered.

Having outgrown the Dutch Boy haircut, I'd entered the age, when left to nature, I didn't measure up. I have to admit to a case of the teenage ganglies topped with a face full of acne, neither easily altered, but more pressing, according to Mother, I needed a PERM. She didn't mention the letters stood for Painful External Rudimentary Metamorphosis.

This torture device came in an innocent box. The contents included bone-like rods with rubber restraints, plastic gloves, a hood, and bottles of caustic fluid meant to burn short straight hair into curly submission. Through many teenage years my blond bob had the look of electrocution.

Later, free of family constraints, my hair magically straightened and grew to my shoulders, grew past the blades and on toward my waist. As well as long hair, I acquired a helmet, blue leathers, and a matching blue Honda motorcycle, a 350cc machine topping out at 110 miles an hour. If nothing else, I thought my poor mother would appreciate the coordinated color scheme.

And then the police—not that I'd been cranking anywhere close to 110. In fact, I hadn't even been speeding, though street racing was my preferred recreation.

"License and registration," one trooper said. "And take off the helmet."

I did as asked, hair blowing over my shoulders, when the other one said, "That'll be twenty bucks."

Many things were wrong with this scenario, but first Mother's voice rang in my head, "See I told you so." So what else had

Mother been right about, the lipstick I didn't wear? Eyeliner? Mascara? Taking a compact to powder my nose? I'd need a suitcase to carry it all and fifteen minutes out of every hour to reapply the useless varnish on my now blemish-free skin. Then there was the girdle. Stockings and other itchy unmentionables. Where does it all end? And at twenty bucks a pop for each infraction against propriety, that could get expensive.

"Not you," said the trooper. He pointed at his partner. "Him. He bet me twenty you weren't a girl."

"Girls don't ride motorcycles," the other one said.

Shows you what he knew, and by extrapolation what my mother knew. This left me free to ignore her advice on make-up, on clothes, and modes of transportation, though not always free of guilt.

E. B. Moore is a metal sculptor turned poet, turned novelist living in Scarborough Maine. Publications: Stones in the Road (*Kirkus starred review 'One of the Best Books of* 2015*'*). An Unseemly Wife. New Eden, A Legacy, a poetry chapbook. *Fellowships: The Vermont Studio Center, The MacDowell Colony, IUD. ebmoore.net*

41 RACKED BY JULIE O'HORA

Racked.

It's a funny thing, having boobs. Sometimes they get you in the room and it's great, 'cause you've worked hard and you deserve to be there. But just as often (maybe *more* often) you get stuck in there while someone you've respected and admired for years stares down your shirt, not listening to a damn word you say.

(Inspired by the A-list agent who insisted the best way to jumpstart my screenwriting career would be to blog about being a hot mom in the suburbs, with lots of sexy selfies.)

Julie O'Hora is a film/TV writer mining the funny from the suck of real life.

42 HIDDEN GIRL BY H. L. RUE

I lived in the Middle East when
I was told of the changes coming,
curves, bumps and bleeding and it was then I first
wanted to hide.

Around me I saw women bundled in
all-encompassing, enveloping
secretive
black material.
It covered them from head to toe.
I coveted their formless shape and
anonymity.
I believed I'd found my answer.

I wanted to hide in there
like they did, acceptably.

In the swish of dark cloths and heady perfume,
only eyes

forthcoming from the blanketed mountain or hill of
    nothingness.
I did not scoff at these women like my expat friends,
who reveled in their own tank tops and short jean
    shorts.
I envied the invisibility the *niqab* and *abaya* afforded
    their wearers.

A visit to a theme park in the States
rattled me when no authority figures appeared
to tell a woman whose butt-cheek had descended
below the hem of her too-short shorts
that she was indecent and her bare shoulders and
visible navel are *haram*, a sinful crime.
Au contraire, these girls were everywhere
while my attire consisted of
long culottes and an extra-large, extra-long t-shirt
in which I tried so hard to hide.

But when we returned,
the women enshrouded in black fabric
came to our Western house parties
unwrapped to reveal
decadent, sleeveless dresses
with short skirts or bare midriffs.
I knew then, even they could not hide completely.

I cannot cover myself like
the Muslim women I admire.
Not in my Christian-values world,
no matter how much
I want to hide.

And even if I could, no textile would grant me the
    obscurity I long for.

Instead I've learned to conceal myself
in plain sight
by repelling advances.

Look at my look just not at me.

Weight gain,
goth clothes,
piss off "don't mess with me" attitude;
all these instantly deflect
male attention.

All unwanted: "All American."

I am so scared of the men.
I am terrified of being "woman" instead of "girl."
I wish my culture had acceptance of the *burqa*.
I just want to hide my body.

*H. L. Rue is an Adult Third Culture Kid
and spent more of her life living outside
the US rather than in her native country.
Currently, she is raising her own TCKs
and navigating reverse culture shock,
having recently returned to the US after
six years overseas with her spouse.*

43 FAT, AND AN OPEN LETTER TO A BARE RAZOR BLADE BY CHRISTINE SAVOY-JOHNSON

FAT

Fat is not synonymous with bad.

The fat girl you see walking down the street; you have no clue how she got that way.

We have things like fat camps and constant bombardment of weight loss commercials and the airbrushed fake magazine covers that rest in our grocery store, hovering just above the plethora of no-no snacks.

Fat is not synonymous with ugly. I am so sick of hearing backhanded compliments like "Wow, you are so pretty, for...you know..." or "Where do you find such cute clothes...in your size?"

Fat is not synonymous with unhealthy habits. "Well, maybe you should cut back on your calorie intake," or "Oh my, don't eat so late." Do you even know my caloric intake? Yeah, I ate a bowl of ramen at eleven last night, but guess what else? That's all my paralyzed stomach has let me eat for the last two days.

Fat is something I am, not who I am, and if you don't know that...

AN OPEN LETTER TO A BARE RAZOR BLADE

I distinctly remember when we met, almost thirty years ago now.

You, all shiny, reflective, and sharp. Everything that I aspired to be; you were so beautiful to me.

I would touch you, all cold and hard like the world around me.

So familiar.

I would always wait a moment; staring at your thin, straight, edge picturing myself standing on it

like a tightrope.

There was so much excitement in that moment, confusion, happiness and shame.

I would lower you to my delicate soft brown skin, lightly press, then stop.

It was a tease, a dance that we did in this fucked-up relationship that we find ourselves in.

I pressed again, left swipe; that meant something different then.

I saw the rush of red, red has always been one of my favorite colors.

So bright and vibrant, yet angry and violent like the scars that you left on the hidden parts of my legs and my arms.

I visited you often in those days.

I found comfort in you and you found a home in me.

Thirty years, thirty years and I just realized what a monster you are.

Now, if there's a snapshot or a commercial, even a quick glimpse of you, my pulse quickens, blood rushes to my cheeks, mimicking the red on my face that you used to leave on my body.

We're not friends anymore, some days I miss you, some days I hate you, some days I praise you, but it's over now.

Never again will I touch you bare naked and far too intimate.

I don't wish to keep company with you anymore, no actually I don't need to these days.

The only way that you're around is hidden inside pretty pink plastic shells that shave the stubble off of my legs, under my arms, and now that I am over forty, sometimes even my face.

I no longer wish to see you, exposed, naked and vulnerable like you used to see me.

Not anymore.

So this is an open letter to that razor blade that used to be such a good companion.

I recognize you now; you're someone I used to know.

I find my release in more productive places. I bleed in public in hopes of helping others, and that leaves no scars upon this body that I finally figured out how to value.

I'm Christine Savoy-Johnson, aka Savage Intellect. I write poetry so that people know that they're not alone in their struggles. My coping mechanism is writing, but only later in life did I realize how cathartic it is to read aloud. Let me inspire you and move you to action.

44 THUNDER THIGHS BY KATHLEEN SLAUZIS

When I was in junior high, those words escaped some nasty teen's mouth as I sat on the grass after school one day. My current boy crush sat next to me as the insulter walked by, and I let the words sink in... I felt the heat rush to my face and looked down. Ashamed.

Thunder Thighs.

Tears of frustration as I am in the fitting room, trying on jeans. Skinny, boyfriend, mid-rise, high waist, a pulling contest of over the thighs and across my stomach. The bigger the waist, the bigger the thigh room. Nothing ever fits right.

Thunder Thighs.

Sitting next to strangers on planes, climbing into car seats, riding on roller coasters; these are all times when I sit awkwardly to avoid having my thighs touch. Don't move. Don't breathe. Don't let others feel how much space I need to be comfortable because of my size. They awkwardly keep away too.

Thunder Thighs.

The blob of shadow on the mat while I'm in downward

dog, my thighs supersized by the sun. Folding legs over legs creating gaps because my thighs can't reach. A place of peace becoming a place of judgment as I feel their eyes watching me struggle. The teacher sympathetically giving me different poses.

Kathleen Slauzis is a cheeky plus-sized geek and transplant from the California beaches to the waves of Midwestern corn. She is a mother of one, lover of arts, and obsessed with good food. This is her first published written work.

PART 6

GRIT & CONFIDENCE

RANDY SUSAN MEYERS

"I think that what I have been truly searching for as a person, as a writer, as a thinker, as a daughter, is freedom. That is my mission. A sense of liberty, the liberty that comes not only from self-awareness but also from letting go of many things. Many things that weigh us down."

—Jhumpa Lahiri

Vector Image by Michele Paccione

In a strange and utterly surprising turn of events, writing my novel *Waisted*, the book which I'd avoided writing for so many years, became the turning point in my life where I found my own grit and confidence.

In *Waisted*, two women who torture themselves and are brutalized by others around weight issues, get caught in the war against women, disguised as a war against fat. While enrolled, with five other women, in an extreme weight loss documentary, they discover self-love and sisterhood as they enact a daring revenge against the exploitative filmmakers.

In the past, I've written novels about a range of issues, from domestic homicide to learning that the man you love has lied for the past forty years, and yet this one, about weight, became the book that flattened me.

Facing how deeply I defined myself by how I looked—my weight, my face, my hair—became a self-examination I'd avoided my entire life. Sure, I knew how marked I was, growing up in a household where beauty meant everything—but understanding the underpinnings of my life and facing them were different. Writers are always asked, is that character you? The real answer, no matter how much we might mumble and deflect, would be this: every character—yes, every character—holds a bit of the author. Whether it be the sadistic trainer hating on women, or the woman terrified to step on the scale, or the mother who can't keep her mouth shut, or the husband judging his wife, or the daughter judging her mother: every character I write dredges up a piece of me.

And letting myself get through that fire, honestly as I could, writing down to the bone of women dealing with their bodies, face, hair, skin, and everything else—that deep dive brought me the totally unexpected gift of grit and confidence.

45 SELF-INDULGENT BY SHEKINAH DAVIS

WINNING ENTRY

Mid-section merry
No meals missed
Muffin top pudge
A hang over the belt,
Enough to grab.

Self-conscious she
Is not, thigh smacking
Like rabid kissers
Fires spark from
So much rub.

Stretch marks
Dark and light
Squiggly and striated
A reminder of
The tiger in her blood.

Beauty marks,
A mole minefield
Bacne, like a
Speckled frog.

There is life
In her scars
Traumatic
Openings
Now sealed
Tight, sutured
In self-love.

In her bare
Naked truth
She stands
Unshaken.

Shekinah Davis was born in Georgia in 1995. She received her BA from Florida State University in 2017, where she obtained a degree in Creative Writing. Currently, she is attending Saint Joseph's University in Philadelphia, completing her MA in Writing Studies. Davis hopes to become a flourishing writer, inspiring many.

46 PHOTO BY VENUS PRADO

WINNING ENTRY

Self-portrait, Venus Prado

As I've gotten older, my facial structure has started to change. I've been reading about it, so I know it's a normal process of aging. The corners of my lips point down now. And I could choose to fret over it and judge myself as "less" than, but you know what—I'm much stronger than that. I show you ME and I love ALL of me.

(Text from the Instagram post that accompanied Venus Prado's winning photo.)

Artist, Writer, Therapist, Mom, Human, Educator. My favorite color is YELLOW. Yes, Venus is my real name. Noah the Cat loves to lay across my body as we sleep together each night. San Antonio is home. My son Cameron is the greatest gift I will leave this world.

47 IF ONLY BY AMY BLANARU

He's holding court.

She's unimpressed. Or at least that's what she wants him to think. It's hot. She tugs her sleeve below her wrist and clutches a worn paperback. There is no air conditioning and she feels sweat drip from her breasts past her belly button. It drips warm and slow, like the tears from her blood-shot eyes. Like the blood from her wrist. But that is gone now, carefully covered by Band-Aids and her sleeve.

The dude with the comb-over from HR drones on about the appearance of impropriety. Dumb people ask dumb questions about ethics. Ethics. *How fitting*, she thinks. She mentally checks out for a second and memory floats into her consciousness. He's on top of her as she lies on her back, stiff as a board. His knees engulf her hips. She looks past him, afraid it will all be a dream if she looks him in the eye. He cups her chin and she can no longer deflect. Looking into her eyes from above, he tells her he is taking a mental picture to retain the moment forever. She nods, afraid she has lost the ability to speak. If only she had rolled over or stopped him from encompassing her. If only. But it was too late. Every pore, wrinkle, and hole in her body had been infiltrated. Every synapse of her brain filled with his chemicals. Every thought in her mind, every beat in her heart, conquered. Every breath she drew in and held tight in her chest. He was in every teeth clench and every toss and turn of failed sleep.

Mr. Comb-Over puts on a PowerPoint about workplace violence. Workplace violence. *Perfect,* she thinks. When he wasn't busy being a court jester for his brethren of sycophants, he had indulged in some workplace violence of his own. *I can't keep going back to these dark places,* he had said, standing between her legs as she sat on his desk. Their exchange had begun simply: flirtatious banter, sharing of books and music. Conversations about favorite artists and upcoming exhibits. If only. If only it had stopped there, but no. Somehow, through entropy or spontaneous human combustion, she was suspended on his desk, legs around his neck, about to come, as he whispered something about her having the Mona Lisa of pussies.

When he went down on her, she glimpsed the tattoo on his arm that read "HATE" and wondered why she always sought out other dark artists. Musicians and songwriters who wrote about chaos.

Screenwriters who told stories of death. A photog whose pictures were all of skid row. And she, with her poems of loss and isolation. When she thought about the jester and the other dark artists, she saw her path with each of them through a cinematic lens in the form of a film reel. In her mind, she cranked the projector into motion, and black and white text and pictures floated by. It wasn't just the tattoo or the film scripts or the skid row pictures that were in black in white; entire memories were devoid of color. The reel winds and the next frame is a split screen. Her naked body looms in black and white on the left side of the screen while the text, *Create Space,* lingers on the right. If only she could blend the two, then maybe she could create space in her heart, and her life would be filled with color. If only she were thin.

Amy Blanaru lives in Boston, MA and is a licensed mental health counselor with a passion for public health. She is also a freelance writer in the process of writing a book of poetry. Her work has been featured in Rebelle Society.

48 BABZ AT THE BARRE BY BABZ CLOUGH

I literally limped into 2018. A week before Christmas, I tore my meniscus. Then, during a visit to my brother's house over the holidays, I caught whatever was going around. By New Year's Day, I had complete laryngitis and a knee brace.

It just had to get better, right?

After the holidays, on my way home from work, I was shuffling through Chinatown when self-pity overtook me. If I fell or got mugged, I could neither run away nor call for help. At fifty-five years old, I felt physically vulnerable for the first time in my life.

I'd always been a high-impact, high-octane kind of person. At six foot two and 180 pounds, ballet and gymnastics got pushed aside early on. In high school gym class, the coach had wanted me on the basketball team, but growing up in a large, dysfunctional family, there was no support for sports even if I had been interested. I lived in a small town and I was always the tallest kid in the class. At one point, I was *the* tallest kid in the school. And no one ever let me forget it for a second. I was teased unmercifully and developed a tough and edgy attitude as a protective mechanism.

Not until my twenties did I start to realize that tall was okay. In my thirties, I started running marathons, in my forties I took up CrossFit, and in my fifties, Muay Thai. I'd found activities I was good at and that made me feel good. But here I was, starting my 56th year, limping and mute. As my orthopedist pointed out, now that I was a woman of a certain age, maybe I should try something a little less stressful on my middle-aged body.

I decided to try something totally new and outside my comfort zone. I'd slowly rebuild the muscles in my legs, improve my balance and posture, and work towards resuming my previous high-impact activities in the future. Without knowing much about it, I decided to try barre. Barre is this weird mash up of ballet and Pilates and booty shaping. (Yes, booty shaping, according to my instructor.) It looked like something I could do until my meniscus healed. It was more strenuous than walking and physical therapy, which was all I'd been able to do for months.

In my first class, I stood in the middle of the mirrored room, and suddenly I was fourteen years old again, freakishly tall and terribly uncoordinated. As a woman, tall is only good if you're a rail-thin model. Or super-coordinated and able to dunk jump shots. But I was neither of those—then or now. I was Gulliver in the land of the Lilliputians. I am not exaggerating when I say I was a foot taller than the instructor and probably double her weight. Standing in front of that mirrored wall, with my Lilliputian classmates, I saw myself as others must see me.

It's not that I don't know I'm tall—I do. But until a complete stranger feels the need to remind me, usually with some unsolicited comment, like "Wow you're really tall," I often forget. It's just who I am, not something I consciously think about every second of every day.

During that first barre class, I had no idea what I was doing. There was all this weird equipment that seemed to serve no purpose but to make me—already regressing to my tortured adolescence—feel even more uncoordinated. There were these squishy balls about six inches across, long black straps, and tiny weights, little 2lb. miniature weights made for miniature people. The weights practically disappeared when I wrapped my long fingers around them. I was used to Olympic lifts and measuring my weights in percentage of body weight, not in 1lb. increments. The bar I was supposed to use for my graceless ballet moves was anchored to the wall at "waist" height, which meant it hit me somewhere below my hip joint. With a 36" inseam, my waist was significantly higher than everyone else's.

I started out in the back row of the class, just as I had stood in the back row as teams were chosen during gym in high school. In the back row, there was less opportunity for anyone to see me in my glorious awkwardness. And I could follow what everyone was doing, because I was clueless about what was going on. Sometimes, when I clenched that little blue ball between my thighs, it would pop out, and in the back row, I could watch where it flew. There was a lot of thigh clenching going on in that class, because we all knew that shapely thighs and booties would lead to life-long success.

I had to keep reminding myself why I was there. I wanted to get strong again. I wanted to stop limping. I wanted to return to CrossFit and running. I didn't really care about a shapely booty or having legs that looked like a dancer's. I wanted knees that didn't hurt and would take me into the next decade and beyond. I realized, after about six weeks, that I didn't really like barre, but I persevered nonetheless. Many of the moves I couldn't do—I hadn't the strength yet. But I kept going, because

I realized as I got stronger and limped less that what I could do in my forties was not necessarily what I should do in my fifties. That just as my thinking had evolved and menopause had changed my body, maybe it was time for my mind to be a bit more open to change as well.

I still want to run. I want to feel that release when my feet are hitting the pavement with every stride but my mind is somewhere else, thinking about a difficult scene in my novel or listening to the sound of the wind in the trees. I fantasize about deadlifting my body weight in a CrossFit class and feeling like an Amazon when I do. I don't fantasize about having an uplifted shapely booty in my sixties. Instead I want my glutes to be strong enough to propel me off the sofa without having to pull myself to a standing position.

I still go to barre. Now I pick a spot in the middle of the room, and the latecomers take the back row. I laugh a little bit to myself when I realize that the petite girl behind me with the shapely booty can't see herself in the mirror because all glorious six foot two of me is blocking her view. And I no longer feel enfeebled or awkward. I don't see a long-term relationship with barre, but for now, it's where I need to be.

Babz Clough lives north of Boston, MA and has been a writer for as long as she can remember. She's finishing her first novel and is working on a collection of short stories about young widowhood. In addition, she regularly participates in StorySLAMs for The Moth *and Mass-Mouth, and she'll be heading to her first* Moth GrandSLAM *in 2019.*

"Am I beautiful yet?"

My fourth-grade body was awkward and unshapely. I still had my baby fat and my chest was just beginning to develop. My back brace from acute scoliosis made it hard for me to lose weight or gain muscle. After all, I could not maintain the label of "competitive dancer" when I was not even allowed to dance.

"Am I beautiful yet?"

My sixth-grade body was uneven and disproportionate. I had little to no shape where my butt was supposed to be and my classmates loved to remind me of it. My chest was still in the "in between a training bra and real bra" phase. My somewhat crooked teeth featured four small metal brackets of braces. I could only acquire four brackets at a time because my orthodontist was worried that too many at once would trigger my Chronic Regional Pain Syndrome. My journey with braces was extended two painful months thanks to the stunted beginning.

"Am I beautiful yet?"

My eighth-grade body was bone. My chest developed, my

butt had shape and my ribs were visible. My braces were all attached and the back of my two front teeth were weak because of the stomach acid corrosion. I did butt workouts religiously. My twelve-hour dance week made them even more strenuous, due to my tired body, but I was committed to having an enviable body. My purging, crying and throwing up routine proved even more exhausting than any workout in the studio. I was one of the lucky group of teenagers who did not struggle with acne. My skin was clear, my body had become a dream for any insecure girl or Instagram model, and my teeth were becoming perfect.

"Am I beautiful yet?"

My sophomore year of high school body was the topic of many conversations. I had the body that ballerinas dream of. I stood at 5'4", possessed long arms, endless legs, a 22-inch waist and the hypermobility disorder, Ehlers-Danlos, which allowed my legs to reach behind my head during *grand battements* and my *développé* to appear to "go on for days." As graceful as it was, my sophomore body was also weak, fragile, and eventually, broken. My L1 and L2 vertebrae literally cracked under the pressure of my intense dance schedule. I was sidelined for an entire competition season. I found this more painful than the double compression fractures at times. I was reunited with the same hard plastic back brace that I had grown to despise in elementary school. I was also reunited with the same insecurity that consumed me in middle school. So, tell me, did my bulimia make me a better dancer? Did my spiraling eating disorder help me feel better? Did my butt exercises help my strength? Did my overwhelming cycle of hating my body solve anything? Did any of it make me "beautiful"?

My senior year of high school body is here. I still get bloated. I still suck in my stomach for pictures and I am still disappointed by what I see in the mirror or scale sometimes.

Even with all these moments of unhappiness, I can say that I am beautiful. My struggles with the mirror, my self-hatred and my embarrassment of my body make me beautiful. The knowledge that I gained through all of the doubts, along with the power to eat a hamburger and keep it in my stomach, are what make me Gabrielle Condren. Bulimia, insecurity, and damages made me, but strength, recovery, and kicking butt define me. So, am I beautiful yet?

Yes.

Gigi (Gabrielle) Condren, 17, is from Wellesley, MA. She will graduate from Cambridge School of Weston this spring and start at The University of Miami in the fall. She has been a competitive dancer for over 10 years.

My hair, like my life,
is in transition.
Tired of living fake,
living quiet,
living as if
I am what men
would think young,
I let the white in.

Beginning at the roots
it melts downward
into waterfalls of snowy,
bubbling joy
between the strands
of tired brunette,
until they merge
like swirling batter,
like cream in coffee,
my own chiaroscuro.

Susan Merrifield Desrocher of SueDesigns® is a Boston-based poet, photographer and writing group facilitator. Susan's mantra is "Illuminate the everyday." She lives that by saluting ordinary local scenes with photo cards and by coaching those in her writing groups to create from seeing the joy and beauty around them.

DISCOMFORT

There it is jabbing at me
That unforgettable feeling
Longing to be something more
Will it be?
There it is again
As if my body is some kind of playground
Praying for well-being
Will it be?
The undeniable fear of the unknown
Will it ever be known?
Will I ever know?
Gnawing at my core
Ripping up my dignity
Will it be?
As yesterday and days before
The mystery goes on

And I live this vivid nightmare again
Will I be?
Will I be?

SELF-ANALYSIS

Lying in a field of conflicted sunflowers really brings
    out the sun's vibrance
Have I ever truly felt whole?
Have I ever actually sought out self-awareness?
The real question presents itself to me in its most
    blissful state, was solitude my goal or was
    wholesomeness?
I continue my journey along the path of self-deception;
But did I ever truly flutter in the fields that lay
    beneath me?
To ponder I must reflect, and to reflect can become
    exhausting
Self-discovery has taught me polyamory is a path to
    wonder within
Is this deception and lust conspiring against my
    latitudinarian will?
Misguided would be an understatement

Ciahna Heck is thrilled to have this opportunity as this is her first time being published in a book. She is highly experienced within the arts as she is trained vocally, in the theater, and in creative writing. She'd like to thank everyone who has believed in her. So much love.

My legs
and my determination
brought me here.

In the wild,
surrounded by unconquerable beauty,
I feel inescapably beautiful.

No matter
my stretch marks,
my scars,
my residual insecurities.

This body,
this imperfect vessel,
has brought me this far.

It has allowed me
to hold

long-awaited babies,
nibble on fresh raspberries,
and listen
to old friends laughing
long past midnight.

It'll carry me forward
step by step by step
into a future
in which my mind
and my spirit
are just as,
if not more,
important than how
I might look
to any outsider
who cannot see
the riches within.

Flawless it is not;
fearless I aim to be
in my pursuit
of a well-lived life.

Julie Henderson was raised on a grain farm in eastern North Dakota. She started writing stories when she was seven. Since graduating from the University of Jamestown with a degree in English, she has traveled extensively, hiked the entire Appalachian Trail, and explored the limits and possibilities of language.

53   THIS IS YOUR LIFE: THE STORY OF A BODY BY PAMELA JOHNSTON

This is your life: You are born into a family with a history. One child has already died. As children, themselves, your parents endured abject poverty. Their greatest fear, now, is a loss of control.

This fear manifests itself in rules. You learn from your sister what happens to people who break them. You become a follower: of rules, authority figures, societal expectations.

This is your life: You grow up hating your body because it does not match the pictures in *Teen* magazine. Your mother suggests eating an apple instead of ice cream. Meanwhile, she makes an apple pie for your father and your brother, then adds a scoop of vanilla on the side.

But at least your mother is not as bad as your friend Michele's. You spend a lot of time at Michele's house because she has a pool. One day Michele's mother brings out squares of orange cake with cream cheese frosting. For Michele, she brings out a plate of sliced tomatoes.

"*You* don't need to be eating cake," she says.

Michele is a size 2.

This is your life: One bad boyfriend after another: the bully, the clinger, the entitled Republican. The list goes on. And just when you've decided that you're done with men altogether, another guy shows up. He's cute and smart and funny. He tells you that you're beautiful.

You know this isn't true. You understand that this is what men say to women. Still, you think he's sweet for saying it.

This is your life: You get married. You fight about ridiculous things: how often to do the laundry, how to load the dishwasher. You do not understand why it's so difficult for your husband to just follow the rules.

But after a while, you get tired of fighting. Who cares how the dishes go into the dishwasher, as long as they do?

This is your life: You get pregnant, and then you lose the baby. You didn't realize how much you wanted a child. Now, you aren't sure you'll ever have one.

Then you're pregnant again, and everything is normal. Until it isn't. Your blood pressure is sky high. The doctor sends you straight from her office to the hospital. You're sent home later, put on bed rest. Nothing is normal. You're angry that your body has failed to do what both your sister's and your mother's bodies have done, seven times, without incident.

Then a beautiful baby girl is born. You are *amazed* at what your body has done.

. . .

This is your life: You get pregnant a third time, while working on your PhD. One of your professors asks, "Was this planned?" You don't think it is any of her business, but that isn't something you can say.

So you shrug. She shakes her head.

"Two kids before you've even finished your dissertation," she says. "You're either really brave or completely crazy."

This is your life: Your daughter comes home from preschool crying because a friend says that her mom is fat. "I don't think you're fat!" she says to you. "I think you're beautiful!"

You tell your daughter that *fat* means lots of different things to different people. You tell her what really matters is that you feel good about yourself.

"Do you feel good about yourself?" she asks.

You know the right answer to this question, but the right answer is not the truth.

This is your life: You finish your PhD and get a job. (Brave, it turns out.) You move your family to Texas, buy a house, settle in. Some years later, you volunteer to chaperone a group of girls from your church on a weekend retreat in the Texas Hill Country.

On Saturday morning, the girls want to join a group that will climb to the cross that's planted on top of a nearby hill. They want you to go along. It's been years since you climbed more than a flight of stairs, but you say yes. You're from Idaho. You've hiked up *mountains*. This, after all, is just a hill.

Halfway up, you realize that you've made a huge mistake.

By the time you get to the top, your heart is beating much too fast. Not BOOM BOOM BOOM, but *bbbbbbbbb*. You're afraid a counselor will have to call for help. EMS will have to carry you down the hill on a stretcher. The girls' parents will have to be called. *Please come pick up your daughter. The chaperone had to go to the hospital because she was too fat.* You would almost rather die than have this happen.

Almost.

So you pray. *God, please help me get off this mountain. I'm sorry I've let myself go. Help me get down from here and I promise, I'll do better.*

You know this isn't how God works. Still, you manage to get off that mountain.

Later, you tell your husband what happened. Then you buy a treadmill. At first, you can barely walk a mile. Then you can walk two miles. Eventually, it occurs to you: maybe you could run.

You hold on to the handrails, afraid you'll fly off. But then you let go.

You are forty years old, and you are running.

This is your life: You're on the way to the mailbox when your next-door neighbor says, "Did you give up eating for Lent?"

You're at the zoo with your family when your daughter says, "You look like such a jock."

On both occasions, you're wearing a pair of running pants and a T-shirt. This is what you wear when you're not at work.

This is your life: Your children grow up and go to college. You go to the gym three or four times a week. You donate the treadmill to Goodwill. Each time you go to the gym, you push yourself a little further. You don't run anymore, thanks to a bad knee, but the elliptical machine still lets you move fast. The stair climber assures you that hill would not be a problem now.

You still don't look like a picture from a fashion magazine, but you don't read those magazines anymore.

You go to the gym because you like knowing your body is capable. You eat an apple because it's good for you. Knowing you're strong, knowing you're healthy, makes you feel beautiful.

This is your life. You lead it.

Pam Johnston is a Professor of English at Texas Lutheran University and the author of a novel, Little Lost River *(University of Nevada Press). Her non-fiction work has been featured in* The Chronicle of Higher Education, Jamie Oliver's Food Revolution, *and elsewhere.* "This Is Your Life" *first appeared on her blog,* She Dwells in Possibility, *which has been syndicated nationally on* The Huffington Post *and* Scary Mommy. *In addition to being a writer and professor, Pam is also a mother, wife, and feminist—not necessarily in that order.*

The blonde tenant is being evicted by the gray. Please move away, Ms. Gray!

The forehead lines are the stairs down to the #11 above the nose my friend Jackie once said gave me a great classical profile.

Someone left two packed bags under my eyes. I wish they'd go on the trip already!

One of the few things thinning are my lips. I was born with one chin, but I picked up another somewhere along the way. Is anyone missing a chin?

Like Nora Ephron said, "I feel bad about my neck." I feel a little less bad, because the skin condition on my neck, Poikiloderma of Civatte, sounds like a glamorous Italian countess. Look that up when you're bored!

The Girls have changed—a lot. They're still pretty perky (so many friends say their girls have gone south). The Girls are bigger, but looser, if you know what I mean. I always wanted cleavage, so there's that. Now, I don't need a push-up bra, but sleeping on my side is problematic. I'm thinking of investing in a boob cushion for side sleepers. Google it, it's a thing!

I realize now that I did not appreciate my abdomen enough. It's taking revenge on me. The first hit was carrying around my ten-pounder. The ten-pounder is now a twenty-three-year-old getting her master's degree from Boston University. My abdomen never recovered. It has the pooch and an apron. Everyone talks about the pooch. Do you know about the apron? It's that loose skin that hangs like an apron. Yeah, now you know. The second hit was right about the time I turned fifty. My upper abdomen, where a six pack is stored, if you have one, started to increase. A layer of fat just showed up one day, replacing the six pack with rolls. All carbs are bad, right?

I gotta say I'm happy to be a pear. At this stage, I carry a bit more junk in the trunk, and my thighs are more thunderous, but research says my ticker is likely to be healthier, and my risk factor for stroke and diabetes is less. Well, ain't that cause for celebration?!

My left knee complains after too many stairs. My right thigh feels numb with bursitis. I did kick Plantar Fasciitis to the curb. I am a Saturday morning yogi now. Stretch, flex, balance, repeat. My chakras are satisfied.

My calves are not the best traveling companions anymore. When the Thai massage lady in Chiang Mai seemed concerned, I knew it was time to do something. I broke down and bought my first pair of compression stockings two years ago. Now I don't leave home without 'em.

I do like my feet. They are still shapely and cute, no bunions, hammer toes, or ugly, yellowed nails. They look positively pretty in sandals with a fresh pedicure.

Next year I'll be fifty-two, only ten years younger than my mom when she died. I know I am healthier than she was. I've never smoked. I try to keep stress at bay. I eat a decent diet, mostly Mediterranean. I don't take any meds, which I think is huge. Could I have exercised more? Probably, but I did okay.

This fifty-one-year-old body feels neither bad, nor good, just different. I feel more comfortable in my skin. I know myself better now. I have learned to listen to myself, trust myself, and allow myself to BE.

Head to toe, I am woman.

I am beautiful.

I am strong.

I am talented.

I am funny.

I am enough.

Barbara is a full-time travel advisor, living in Florida. In her 29-year career, she has visited 30 countries. She enjoys reading, singing, music and dreams of having a cabaret show someday. Barbara has a carefree spirit. She is married with one daughter in grad school.

I toggled between "Lark" and "X-Pro II," trying to get the perfect photo filter for my Instagram post. The Lark setting softened the lines on my face, but the X-Pro II really made my blue eyes pop, and my eyes are my best feature—at least that's what I've been told.

I settled on Lark, because it didn't look *too* filtered and gave me the appearance of "natural" beauty. Didn't want to look too made-up, or like I do in real life. Satisfied (except for the way my elbow was bent at a weird angle, making my upper arm look chubby), I posted my pic. The emoji comments that began to trickle in made me feel like I made the right choice. Made me feel like I looked good enough.

Looking good enough. Every. Damn. Day. I remember in fifth grade, the boys would taunt me on the playground: "Roses are red, violets are black, why is your chest as flat as your back?" I remember Jody Simmons telling me my nose was so pointy I could slice a loaf of bread. I remember my first dance in seventh grade, when someone in the eighth grade popular group called me a slut because my bra straps were showing.

Women are very familiar with this deep level of exposure. And not just from the cruelty of puberty. It's everywhere—from catcalls on the street to comments from your own family.

Most of my life, I was considered too thin. "Don't you feed this girl?" Sitting on my grandpa's lap: "Your butt is so bony, are you sure you're Italian?"

I am petite. This is true. My hips are narrow, my waist and legs are short. I shopped in the Junior's section until I was twenty-five. Before I had children, my bra size was "Nearly A." My mom is also petite, only thicker and with an actual chest. I watched my mom obsess over her figure for years, yo-yo dieting for as long as I can remember. She's currently on the intermittent fasting fad diet—where you eat only during an eight-hour window and fast for the remaining sixteen hours. As with every diet she's on, when she stops by my house, she grabs a handful of mixed nuts and shoves them in her mouth, while mumbling about her cheat day.

At thirty-seven, with two kids, my petite frame still looks best in short pants, but definitely needs a wider waist. So, where I was once considered too little, I now feel too big. Hernia surgery left a scar down my midsection, with the stretch marks from my two pregnancies puckered into the center—I jokingly dubbed this scar my personal San Andreas fault line. I despise it every time I consider my previous bikini-wearing years. I love it every time I consider its strength. This back-and-forth is a common occurrence.

Sono Bello. My browser history would probably show a search of this phrase at least 227 times. I can't stand the muffin top that makes it impossible to wear the clothes I like. The saggy skin that makes me not feel sexy even though my husband's caresses tell me otherwise.

The love/hate, strength/shame struggle is real. Do I save up the money and get a mommy makeover? (Those once Nearly

As are now Droopy Bs.) Or would that money be better spent on a family vacation? Do I accept my body for what it is? Do I see the flab and flaws as testaments to my womanhood? Or do I smooth away the lumps and lines, like my Lark filter does? To feel pretty, and young. And sexy. Boy, do I wish I could rock a bikini again.

Then the internal dialogue: *Of course, I can wear a bikini. It's my body.* Don't you remember that meme going around Facebook last summer—Every body is a bikini body? But if I did get surgery—I would feel amazing. But would it be shrouded in a different kind of shame—the one that says, "I'm fake"?

Sigh. This round and round gets me sometimes. I'm most at peace with my body when I'm present, in the moment, and having fun with family and friends.

I think of my sons and their relationships with their bodies. Of how they will think of the girls and women in their lives. I think of how my relationship with my own body affects them. When Grandma is over and she complains about feeling fat as I prepare dinner, I pull her aside to ask her to think of how those words may affect her grandsons—I tell her how hearing her say them *my* whole life has affected me. She understands for their sake and bites her tongue. I don't think she can allow that softness for herself. She may hush her outward criticism, but I'm sure her inner dialogue still churns.

I have to practice what I preach. When I look in the mirror, I must remember that I judge myself much more harshly than other people do. I am healthy. My youngest son often pats the poochy part of my belly, noting that's where he came from and declaring it an excellent pillow.

For now, I find acceptance of myself through my relationships and my lifestyle choices. I like to stay active. I have a great job. My glasses are cute. My sons are sweet, smart, and funny.

My future self may find acceptance through different avenues, such as having a surgically enhanced body. I may have a completely different body and mindset. I may not.

Either way, I am allowed to be me. I deserve to be happy in my body. Self-confidence is beautiful.

Last week, I posted pictures of my sons and me on a summer day, and my cellulite was showing. The likes came in— just as they would if I had posted a more discreetly posed picture, my elbow at the right angle, and the filters at their finest. Regardless of the ways we display ourselves in an over-exposed social media world, I realize it's me they like.

And it's me I like.

Nikki McCoy loves living in the Pacific Northwest and often succumbs to the following cycle (which she blames on the rain): Read. Write. Rest. Repeat. When she's not caught in that loop, Nikki can be found in the garden with her husband and two sons, and their chickens, Hen Solo and Princess Layer.

I suppose you could say my trauma started with my brush with death. At eleven years old, a vicious front-end collision resulted in some surface injuries for sure, but the deeper ones would be my undoing.

For starters, my childhood was over. Kaput. Never to be seen again. Because as much as I could play and run about like a normal kid, deep down I knew what lay ahead. Beyond the school, the sports, college, marriage, having kids. Beyond it all was death. And death didn't give a fuck about any of it. Death's over in the corner watching you live, watching you work, watching you screw, all the while sitting in wait for the chance to rip it all away. So yeah, I wasn't a kid anymore.

In a deeper sense, an issue was missed that has continued to plague me ever since. I had been sitting in the front seat, reclined back while my mother was driving. The EMTs recovered me in the back seat with a compound ankle fracture and a mangled collarbone. However, my back went unchecked and it became progressively worse over the years.

The deepest cut was the slow and painful realization that

my metabolism was out of whack and I would continue to watch the pounds go up, and up, and up. In high school, I briefly had an eating disorder. I tried to eat as little as I could. Going to bed and hearing my stomach yearning for something other than iceberg lettuce. Eventually, I stopped. For the mere fact that I really liked food and I hated myself anyway, so why care anymore? Take it a step further. Just hate yourself. Challenge accepted. Self-hatred acquired.

I was always the funny fat friend in the group. Boys didn't go after me. I was the girl you saw as your best friend, not someone to date. Then college happened, and it was more of the same. More loneliness and self-loathing. Attempts to get healthy saw me achieve a seven-minute mile. I hated running. But I forced myself to run because I needed to lose weight. I didn't.

My vicious self-loathing and depression manifested itself in self-medicating with food. I ate my feelings. No fucking wonder I wasn't losing weight. I hated myself and I ate my feelings. Eating all the hate. Chip after chip, ice cream, cookies, pasta a mile fucking high, covered in melted cheese.

Trauma decided it didn't have enough of a presence in my life. Needed to make itself known. At twenty-one-years old, I had my first sexual encounter. And by that, I mean more than a kiss and a fondle. While I drunkenly went in and out of consciousness, a freshman frat boy put my hand down his pants and used my hand to stroke himself. I hid the whole experience away, but it continued eating me up and tearing me apart, day after day.

For a while, I tried again. I tried to care. I tried to make an effort. Seeing no success, I reverted to more self-loathing, eating more pasta piles. I drank more. I associated with people who drank more. I started smoking again. Although I had smoked in my early college years, it was a rare occurrence. I eventually became a full-blown smoker. I stopped caring. But then...

You're seeing a pattern here, yes? I tried again, that is, until an additional trauma forced its way in.

I was raped. November 23, 2016. The night before Thanksgiving. So that holiday is always a nice reminder. The whole self-loathing thing added a new fucking layer. Fuck it. Fuck caring. Hate my body anyway, so let's hate it even more.

But as my therapist pointed out, that isn't exactly a great way to live your life. You have to try. Especially if you want to be happy. So, I decided to start with baby steps. Online dating. The proverbial lamb slicing myself open for the wolves to slaughter.

I met a guy. I had no intention of falling head over heels in love with him, but here we are. From the very beginning, he respected my trauma. He respected who I was, and who I wanted to be. At 210 pounds, I couldn't believe he found me attractive at all. Not when he was fit AF. But what he helped me realize was that I could be the person I wanted to be. To stop the self-loathing and the hate eating. That I could be healthy and happy and as fit. That the passion I had to improve myself was supported by someone who reminded me to eat better and held my hand while I cried over food, because that happened a lot. I mean, like a lot. A lot, a lot. I cried over peanut butter more times than I can remember or would care to admit. Because watching what you eat is hard. But you have to, if you want to get healthy.

And I did it. I made strides. I lost weight. I started to have more pride in my body because I had put in the hard work. I could see my muscles getting stronger because of my efforts. And when you get closer to your dreams, closer to the person you want to be, it becomes an addiction. I'm not done working towards becoming the person I want to be. It will be a contin-uous journey, because I will always choose to be better, to improve myself.

The self-hatred doesn't go away easily. It's a harder fight to fix your inner voice. She's pretty damn nasty. But every day is a choice. And every day I try to choose love.

Writer. Reader. Artist. Hogwarts alum. Nap enthusiast. Coffee expert. Holder of tea parties. Whovian. Alliteration addict. Can often be seen making meandering journeys through her mind in search of something profound. If cranky, approach quietly, offer either caffeine or chocolate. Lives in Michigan with her partner, Scott and dog, Tasha.

57 SOFT BY RAE NOBLE

I can remember feeling my stomach after my son was born, soft, rippling, fleshy, supple; a stretched and exhausted abdomen, trembling with my steps, laughing, delightful, abundant. Softer than everything except my son. Never before had I felt something like this on my own body, a body I had halfheartedly trained for a dozen sports over a hundred months. I think I always, deeply knew that I never wanted rock, never wanted washboard, never wanted to touch myself to feel a stoic and frozen structure. My body as a flower, gentle and transient, moving with the wind and my pulse and my stride. My body as a leaf, not a branch; a melody, not a metronome; an organism, not a machine.

Rae Noble is an artist and art therapist living in the Midwest. Her favorite creative practices currently include writing nonfiction and poetry, learning sign language with her small family, connecting with other mother-artists, and brewing kombucha.

58 DESPITE THE NOSE ON MY FACE
BY JENNIFER "JAY" PALUMBO

It was a beautiful, crisp autumn day as the sun streamed through the family room window. I was in the house where I grew up, sitting on the floor coloring with my niece. It was a peaceful moment, and as she and I decided on the right shade of yellow to color Winnie the Pooh, I noticed my father looking at us. I thought to myself, "He must be thinking what a lovely moment. His daughter and granddaughter coloring together in the family home." I smiled at him. He looked at me and said, "I was just thinking...," as he put down his cup of decaf coffee, "if you got a nose job, it would really help your appearance."

To be clear, my father and I are close, he's a loving dad, I adore him, and I harbor no ill will at this sentiment. If anything, I wish he had a censor button, but I think we all wish that for our parents, don't we? And I DO have a bump on my nose, so while I thought he was taking in a family portrait moment, he was actually taking in MY portrait.

Also, in his defense, I was in my mid-twenties at the time, single and a stand-up comic. While not a cause for alarm, to my somewhat traditional Italian Roman Catholic family, the fact that I was not married yet and spent my time telling jokes was mortifying.

As a Catholic Italian, your life is a series of christenings, weddings and funerals. At every wedding (and there were many), I had to politely tolerate being hounded by several aunts and uncles asking, "When are you going to be next? When are you going to be next?" I found they were not as tolerant when I asked them the same questions at funerals.

Basically, my father, as he put it bluntly in one of our phone conversations, wanted me to "get married already" so he didn't have to worry about me. If, perhaps I got a nose job, it would help my appearance, someone would marry me, and then my dad could go back to drinking caffeinated coffee again.

To make matters worse, my manager would express similar sentiments about my appearance only a month or two after this incident.

My manager, we'll call him "Mr. Asshole" (not his real name), had several comics/writers that he managed. He arranged for all of us to perform at a club in Manhattan and invited industry to attend. Two agents were there from William Morris, which, if you know anything about the entertainment world, is a highly respected agency.

As legend has it (and by legend, I mean Mr. Asshole's assistant who told me the story two days later, when he was drunk), the William Morris agents apparently said complimentary things about me and my performance to Mr. Asshole after the show. However, Mr. Asshole responded with, "Jennifer? Oh yeah, she's great and all, but a better writer than anything else. She's clearly not attractive enough to be on television."

So, let's recap, shall we? My manager, whose job it was to represent me, and my father, who by virtue of his role, should think I'm sugar and spice and everything nice, were both in agreement that my visual appearance needed help. There was also a homeless man on 86th Street that one time who told me I was ugly, but that seemed a little less personal.

I also want to take another moment to mention that if you don't know what I look like, you must be picturing a witch with a hook nose who lives in a bell tower. While I absolutely have my flaws and insecurities, if you saw a picture of me, I'm neither gorgeous nor heinous. In retrospect, it was more my circumstances at the time; single, unmarried, and on stage in front of people, that opened the floor up to votes on my appearance.

Still, when two men you respect are looking at you and seemingly saying, "Meh," it can get to you. So, I did something I never thought I'd do: I booked an appointment to see a plastic surgeon. It was some hot shot doctor on the Upper East Side and, try as I might, I could NOT get any of my friends to go with me for moral support. All of them gave the same reason, too: They were worried the doctor would look at them and tell them what they needed to fix. My friend, Karen, said, "He'll take one look at my double chin and forget all about your nose!"

As I sat in the exam room waiting for the doctor, I looked at the pictures of all the delighted customers. Of course, they were happy! It looked like all of their smiles were glued to *make* them look happy.

His entrance into the room was nothing short of dramatic. It was very grand, as if to say, "I'm here to save you from your genetic curse!" Before we could even exchange pleasantries, he was immediately studying my face.

"For the record, people pay me a lot of money to have your lips," he said.

"Uhhhhhhh. Thank you."

That IS one of the things I do have going for me. I have Angelina Jolie-like lips. What I love about this is that in third grade, the kid who sat behind me in class, John McDonald (his real name, and I hope he reads this), used to make fun of me constantly for having "big lips." He called me "horse lips." I'd love to hunt his ass down now and give him a note from the plastic surgeon. Suck on that, John! But I digress. The lips comment was the last positive thing the doctor said to me.

"I can see the aging process has begun," he said, while looking at my forehead.

I almost burst out laughing. I was twenty-six at the time.

From there, it went downhill. He talked about breaking my nose and inserting some foreign object in to the tip of my nose as my nose points "downward" somehow. He also said I would absolutely need a chin implant to balance off the nose. I guess everything in my face was pointing down? Doesn't gravity do that?

When I expressed that I didn't think I needed THAT much work done, the doctor asked, "What do you do for a living?" I told him. He said, "Well, I wouldn't come to a comedy club and tell you how to do your job!" and then he left as quickly as he came in.

Here I am... a stand-up comic, and I'm now beginning to think it's my actual face that may be a punchline.

After enduring a twenty-minute barrage of "Here's everything wrong with your face," I was led into another room where a woman with the enthusiasm of a DMV worker took photos. She then showed me on a computer screen what I would look like "after," if I let Doctor Personality do all the things he wanted to do.

I gasped. Truly. And I instantly thought two things:

1. I look beautiful.

2. I can't do this surgery.

Honest to God—even I'm shocked about number two. Especially after thinking number one. My logic was, if I had the surgery, and I met someone, and they fell in love with me, I would always wonder if they would have loved me "before" with the bump and all.

There are MANY reasons why people have plastic surgery. Some do it for others and some genuinely do it for themselves, and I respect that. And I think that's part of what my issue was. When I reflect back, I never actually noticed anything wrong with my nose, face, chin, or anything else, until others mentioned it, so I wouldn't be doing it for myself. What sucks is that ever since that fateful appointment, I notice it all now. Still, not enough to do anything about it.

Ideally, this would be the part where I would say that I learned to think I was beautiful despite these flaws, but I can't exactly say that. It's more that I've accepted this is how I look. I don't LOVE it, but I can work with it. And I did end up meeting and marrying someone who thinks I'm beautiful despite whatever may or may not be wrong with my appearance. He's also a comic, so luckily, we have a sense of humor about it all.

I'm also happy to report that my dad was proud to walk me down the aisle and, even though I finally got married, he STILL worries about me, so really, the joke is on him!

Jennifer "Jay" Palumbo is a freelance writer, stand-up comic, infertility/women's health advocate, and author of the blog, The 2 Week Wait. *Her articles have been included in places such as* Time *magazine,* The Huffington Post, *and* ScaryMommy, *and she's been featured on CNN, NPR, BBC and in the documentary* Vegas Baby.

She stands in the shadows
Shedding silent tears
Suffering from unnoticed pain
The eyes of the clowns surround her
Yet, they are oblivious to her despair
They are blind to what is really going on inside of her
Will anyone notice the darkness within her?
Can't anyone see it...?
Can't anyone feel it...?
Can't anyone sense it...?
Surely there has to be someone that can help her
Surely there is someone out there who can guide her to
    the light so that she may see
So that she may see the goodness within her
So that she can recognize the beauty that she holds
So that she may see her strength and rise above her
    crushed soul
She has spent too many lost moments degrading herself
    due to others' insensitive behaviors

She has spent too many lost moments dealing with
    abuse from others
She has spent too many lost moments crying after being
    called ugly, stupid and fat
Fear guided her through most of her life
She could not shake the despair
She could not face her fear
She could not realize that it was SHE who could help
    herself all along

Tianne began writing at age 5 with a Haiku. She has since turned that passion into creating Zines and creating daily. Taking inspiration from life experiences she pours her heart out in words. Once hidden words are now shared with hopes that they may inspire others.

60 YEAH, SO I'M A LITTLE AFRAID OF MY SCALE BY ALISA SCHINDLER

I'm mostly naked and anxious as I study myself in the mirror, grabbing at a "love handle" that I clearly don't love. Turning my body from one side to the other, I try to convince myself that it's not as bad as I think, that I'm okay. But five minutes later, when I step on that scale, the number tells me that, in fact, I am not okay. That even with my exercise and relatively controlled eating habits, I have gained three pounds since the last time I got on the scale, just a week ago.

It's 6:45am, and even though I want to cry just a little with disappointment, I'm too tired. Besides, I'm a mom, which means there's no time for wallowing. There is breakfast to make and laundry to flip and the day is starting no matter how I feel or look. Yet, I already know that there will be a lingering cloud over this day that would not be here had the number on the scale been the "correct" one, the one that allows me to breathe easy and feel comfortable with myself.

Being hyper-focused on three pounds seems ridiculous, and as I sip my coffee, I tell myself that over and over again. But with all the life stresses and being (cough cough) middle aged, maintaining my weight has become one of the things I need to control to keep myself balanced.

I have never been a girl who could eat whatever she wanted. My diet is based on a lot of calculations and tradeoffs, healthy food trends and an on-again, off-again love affair with Weight Watchers. On top of that, I have exercised regularly for over twenty-five years. Still, it's a constant struggle for maintenance, which has only gotten harder with age. And it's strongly tied to my mental health as well. Somehow, everything today, from my patience with the kids to dealing with my ill father, will just be a touch harder.

Aging isn't easy. Not that anyone said it would be. There are wrinkles, sags, and plenty of "What the hell are those?" moments that, like childbirth, you really don't understand until you are screaming, I mean experiencing, it for yourself. But as my grandmother used to say, "It beats the alternative." And she was right. There's nothing to do but keep plugging along. Which is why I'm going to quit moping and start the day with a run (okay, a slow jog); it will be good for my head and body, and will make me feel a little better about myself when I'm done.

Every day, there are ups and downs. Birthday cakes and double scoops. The tight-lipped teen you worry about. The middle child who knows how to push your buttons. The unreasonable boss. That bottle of wine you had to share with your bestie. The aging parent who drives you nuts. I'm there with you trying to appreciate the good things in life while still trying to keep a healthy balance on the crazy. Some days I succeed, and some days, like today, I know I need to work a little harder.

So as much as I'd like to say *screw you* to my lifelong nemesis, the scale, our dreaded weekly showdowns keep me in check. Like it or not, in a few days I will step up again, just as naked emotionally as physically, and hope that when I open my eyes and squint down at the number, I see some positive results.

That moment of truth never ceases to be scary, but I refuse to hide from it.

My front door is open. The air is crisp, and the sun is shining. I am strong. I am beautiful. I am doing the best I can. And I am off and running.

Alisa Schindler is a mom of three boys and wife to Mr. Baseball. She schleps children, burns cupcakes and writes essays that have been featured online at the New York Times, Washington Post, Kveller, Woman's Day, Parents, Good Housekeeping *and* The Well *by* Northwell Health. *On the side, she writes sexy suburban mystery novels available on Amazon. Find out more about her at* alisaschindler.com.

61 OPTICS MANAGEMENT BY LAURIE VALLAS

As I raced down the stairs, desperate to catch the bus, I whizzed past my father as he sat calmly at the kitchen table enjoying his morning coffee. Amidst the frenetic racket in my head, I heard him say, "Oh dear—when will you realize you were built for comfort—and not for speed..."

This was not the first seemingly innocuous remark I managed to internalize over forty-plus years. I continue to work on both believing, and accepting, that such sentiments were innocent in intent.

Of the many beliefs I developed, body confidence was not among them. In fact, not only did I participate in the sport of self-deprecation; I earned my way into the varsity league.

My indoctrination into what I would describe as "optics management" began in childhood; my long hair was suddenly cut short like the Olympic figure skater, Dorothy Hamill—so that I, too, could skate like a champion. This conveniently both boosted my confidence and eliminated the need for my mother to wrestle with a hairbrush every morning.

When my childhood skating passions waned, and my interests turned towards teenaged boys, I was encouraged to grow my hair all one length again—like Jacqueline Kennedy. Of course, this was in preparation for looking the part of Ivy League arm candy. However, when my post-high school future did not include matriculation at Radcliffe, bangs were in order.

Adding to such dilemmas, my fair Irish body was covered in freckles—an intolerable embarrassment for which I desperately sought a remedy. All my babysitting money was spent on Porcelana, a cream that eliminated age spots. I went to bed each night plastered in the stuff...until my mother found the empty jars in the trash and, as the Irish say, "laughed her leg off," as she told my aunts about the determined depigmentation effort to conceal my heritage.

In addition to my hair and skin woes, was the matter of breast development. Initially, I was afraid they wouldn't grow at all, and I used to sneak into my mother's top dresser drawer and try on one of her bras and pray that one day it would fit. Then, to my amazement, and seemingly overnight, my breasts began to grow faster and shamefully larger than those of my peers. Breasts the size of mine did not belong on a young teenaged body. I chalked it up to the power of positive thinking and, of course, prayer. Prayer was good, right? Yes. But...whoa.

I unfairly blamed some of my body-dysmorphia partly on the 'influencer' of my time, Margaret, Judy Blume's fictional character, who introduced me to that 70's mantra:

"I must, I must, I must increase my bust..."

A darker, more pivotal moment in reclaiming my power to live my life on my terms occurred one night as I lay in bed feeling hopeless, yet simultaneously determined to fight back against the constant pressure to "look appropriate." Developing an eating disorder or inventing an addiction to drugs or alcohol seemed like plausible ways to distract, deflect and regain control. Mental debates ensued, such as, "If I became anorexic...vomiting might wreck my teeth," and "I could become a drug addict...but then drugs are kind of expensive," and "If I killed myself...I'd never get to go to prom." I am forever grateful for whatever rational wisdom prevailed that talked me out of going down one of those paths. Thank God I overcame my temporary, illogical, teen-aged drama and realized that any attempt to get back at people for hurting me—would involve hurting myself more.

I decided I wasn't having any of that.

My body confidence muscle gained strength when I became able to deflect remarks such as, "You'd probably be happier if you were thinner" by replying, "No, I'd actually be happier if you would stop commenting on my body."

Over the years, my body has periodically expanded and contracted like an overnight bag; sometimes everything fit in easily—other times I wrestled to zip it closed without it bursting at the seams. In my mid-thirties, I went to live overseas for a while. I was feeling healthy—with enough room in my heart and body to believe I was finally capable of carrying what I really wanted, a child. However, the void left by a miscarriage was filled with a decade-long rage and resentment towards my body for not producing the children I had so desperately expected.

My father offered this wise saying during my recovery process: "Blessed are they who expect nothing, for they shall never be disappointed." While that provided some comfort, a quote from Sri Chinmoy resonated more: "Peace begins when expectation ends."

I have both loved and loathed this "container" that carries all of "me" around, yet it took witnessing the surreal deterioration of my parents' health to be able to make peace with my "pieces," and to be grateful to have them all, in working order, and to nurture every aspect of myself.

Everything is becoming softer now—especially my perspective. I have recently let go of nearly forty pounds; leaving lots of overstretched skin that used to house all that armor. There are a lot more lines across my neck, little pouches that accentuate my jowls, and a crepe-like texture on the back of my hands. But this is mostly just noticeable when I'm wearing my glasses and I frequently end up using them as a headband anyway. Monet was on to something when he decided to focus on the impression of light dancing across his horizon versus the exacting element of detail. Also, things appear blurred as you rush past them—glasses or not.

As I head into the next decade of my life, I often reflect on the claim that I was born three weeks late, and some would argue that I haven't caught up since. I am approaching a stage in my life where, more and more, I resist rushing. Instead, I am allowing life to evolve and unfold at a slower pace. After all, what's the hurry? Gandhi was right, there is more to life than increasing its speed.

For the record though, I did catch that bus...

Laurie is a multi-passionate connector, heartist and voracious wordsmith whose creativity emerges in the vespertine hours. Curious about everything, she loves facilitating the excavation of stories and is drawn to projects that create meaningful legacies. Current plans and projects are updated on Facebook: Laurie Vallas – Author and please join the @theheartifacts movement on Instagram!

REMEMBER THAT GIRL?

High school, sometime in the late 80's
Her ass was as big as her 300-pound sister's
The back of her hair as nappy as the family dog's ass
So pale, looked like two burnt holes in a blanket staring
      at you
With googly turkey eyes bulging from a face too small
And lips so thick you could lick them, stick her to
      the wall
And she'd hang there silently for hours
The smile never really making it to her eyes
Remember now?

Yeah, she's still the same.

PERSPECTIVES

The thing about them?
They get skewed and screwed.

Lovely long hair doesn't matter
When they have to get to the brain
The repair resulting
In an Elmer Fudd noggin
Laced with angry red scars
Housing a sump pump

A tiny waist won't matter
Nor a trimmed bikini line
Should they need tear into your womb
To free your unborn

The shapely legs
Once inspiring cat calls and whistles
Won't be bared to reveal
More scars and mechanical parts

But you'll still shy away from those images
As much as you pampered and attended your body
Attempting to present for judgment your best form
You'll nourish instead
The beauty of your survival
And then you will look into the mirror
With a gentle smile

Hope lives in the deep wood outside D.C. with Saint Paul and The Biskuit, their dog. On any given day, y'all may find her developing recipes using locally grown produce and meats, advocating for the marginalized and medical marijuana rights, or bedridden from complications due to too many brain surgeries. But word weaving allows for the grooviest of arm chair travels...come along!

63 BOOB JOB REGRETS: IN APPRECIATION OF YOUR PREVIOUSLY SMALL CHEST BY DENSIE WEBB

I've wished for bigger boobs ever since I realized at about age fifteen that my A cups were all I was going to get. My "condition" is a genetic hand-me-down from my mother.

Padding was an option ("falsies" as we called them then), but when I was single and dating, there was always that moment of truth. My least favorite memory was of the guy who, as I exposed myself both literally and figuratively said, "You have really small breasts." Really? I'm shocked, but thanks for bringing that to my attention. The perfect rejoinder, of course, would have been to comment about his shortcomings. But, unfortunately, he had none. On a scale of 1-10, he was an 11, maybe a 12, now that I think about it. Probably why he was so arrogant.

Then there was the guy who, bless his pea-pickin' heart, thought he was being complimentary, when he offered up this unsolicited comment, "I like small breasts," as if he was preemptively soothing my feelings of inadequacy. It felt like a slap in the face. Just imagine if I had offered up a similar comment after assessing his attributes. "Gee, I love small penises."

THE BRALESS PHASE

Boob Job Regrets: When You Miss Your Previously Small Breasts. I went through a phase in the '80s when I figured, why wear a bra? (In fact, another wonderfully sensitive person of the male persuasion had asked me that exact question.) So, I began thinking, what is it exactly I'm trying to support here? But my braless phase ended when I realized that the guys in the mailroom at work were staring like Beavis and Butthead (remember them?) whenever I bent over, and my loose top gave a panoramic view of what (little) was underneath. Men.

Breast implants were not as common then. I did mention it to my husband a few years ago, but he let me know I was too old for such nonsense. Thanks, Hon. To his credit, it never seemed to bother him. I do remember once, shortly after he came to this country from Israel, and before his English had reached the advanced level, he looked at me while I was changing and said, "You're so sneaky." Translation: "You're so skinny." I have a feeling he might have been referring to more than my rib cage, but I didn't pursue it.

Men have their own size issues, but the discrepancy is far less obvious than it is for women. While men can make themselves feel incredibly inadequate, obsessing over the difference of an inch or two, women get to compare massive side-by-side differences that are pretty much out there for the world to see.

I've heard really large-breasted women say it's a curse, not a blessing, and I've known a couple who had to resort to the messy and quite painful business of breast reduction surgery. Given a choice between that and my puny chest, I'll stick with what I was given. Still, almost any small-breasted woman will tell you that the other end of the spectrum is a curse as well. Clothes never fit well, especially dresses and swimsuits. Few clothes are made for bodies with a top that's two sizes smaller than the bottom.

THE VICTORIA'S SECRET DRESSING ROOM

My daughter was spared my fate. And, as ridiculous as it may seem to the women who actually have something to fill out a bra, I am thrilled for her. When she was in high school, I went with her to Victoria's Secret to shop for a swimsuit. As I waited outside the door while she changed, I saw women of all shapes, sizes and ages entering and exiting dressing rooms with all manner of underthings. I overheard one woman ask the salesgirl, "Do you have this push-up in a 34 Double D?" Say what??

Even the salesgirl hesitated for a second and said, "I'll check, but I doubt if we carry it. Usually if you're that 'blessed' you don't need anything to enhance it." Or something to that effect. She definitely used the word "blessed." I looked down at my own chest and thought, I must have been absent the day they were handing out the boobie blessings.

When my daughter emerged from the dressing room to model her bikini for me, I was amazed and relieved that I had to tell her, "You're hanging out of that top. You need a bigger size."

ANOTHER SURPRISE

A few years after I saw for certain that I hadn't passed on my boob genes, I had another surprise. This one not so pleasant. I developed breast cancer. (Oh, the irony.) Squeezing my tiny bits of breast tissue into those torture racks called mammograms had always resulted in the "all clear." But, it turns out, breast tissue, even breast tissue as limited as mine, can grow bad cells out of the range of a mammogram.

My breast cancer took up residence in space that could hardly be classified as breast tissue at all. I was lucky, though—stage 1, no chemo. Lumpectomy was tried, but it was no go. Precancerous cells were abundant. A second attempt at a lumpectomy to avoid a mastectomy was a failure, so a mastectomy was my third and last option. I'm not sure I even realized at the time the lengths I was clearly willing to go to save my much-maligned breast.

On the first visit to the plastic surgeon, I was asked, "Do you want to go bigger?" I'd be lying if I said I wasn't just a wee bit excited over the prospect. Despite the cancer thing and my age, it kind of felt like I was finally getting my boobie blessing. My right boob was scooped out like a melon, keeping the external skin and nipple and implants were "installed" on both sides. Five surgeries later (long story) they're a bit lopsided, and sag unevenly, but with a bra, my clothes fit better. When it was all done and I had healed, I felt positively voluptuous. My husband marveled at how natural it felt (on the left side, not my oddly misshapen scooped-out melon on the right). My friends nodded in approval at my new and improved profile.

Was it worth it?

I think you know the answer to that question. If I could go back and undo the cancer, undo the surgeries and everything that comes with having cancer, including a medication I must take that is designed to sap whatever estrogen I might have left, I'd gladly give back my bigger B cups for my previously healthy bitty boobs any day of the week. So, as the sage saying goes, "Be careful what you wish for." You never know exactly how your wishes might come true. Wish for thinner thighs, fewer aches and pains, fewer gray hairs and you just might get your wish, but not quite in the way you imagined.

I've decided to work at accepting whatever physical deficits —real and imagined—that I develop as I age, including my larger, but lopsided, B cups.

Densie Webb (not Denise) has been a freelance nonfiction writer/editor for over 20 years. She is the author of two novels (working on #3), is an avid walker (not of the dead variety), drinks too much coffee, and has a small "devil dog" that keeps her on her toes.

64 HIDING IN PLAIN SIGHT: A TRUE STORY OF WEIGHT LOSS BY SEEDY WILKINS

I've been fairly silent about my journey. It has been a long, arduous one, and I've finally decided that it's time to break my silence. I spent twenty years of my life living as a plus-size woman. I look back at photos taken over those twenty years, and I see the misery and pain. Yet, what I've realized from losing this weight is that there was also an armor, or shield, that came from that plus-size. It's finally time to tell my story.

At my heaviest weight, I tipped the scales at just over 325 pounds. In fact, my doctor at the time joked about calling the Broncos to add me to their roster if I gained any more weight. I bounced from diet to diet, trying to lose weight, while secretly sabotaging myself.

I began seeing a therapist in 2011, because I knew I was sinking and needed help. Within six months, I was ready to face a bigger fear, my kidney disease. I finally saw my nephrologist in February of 2012. As I sat there that morning, I received some hard news. My nephrologist looked at me and said, point blank, "If you don't lose weight, you're going to die. You are killing yourself, and only you can fix it." I had been prescribed cocktail after cocktail of pain pills following a bad car accident, which sent my kidneys into stage four failure. I had to purge my body of all pills, live healthier, and most importantly, I had to lose weight. He then wrote out a referral for a dietitian, and a surgery consult. I was suddenly confronting a fear bigger than the one that had kept me heavy. I had lived through my rapes and abuse, I had built a shield, but now I had to continue to live, because my fear of death and leaving my children was worse.

I agonized over the decision to see a dietician. I had no desire to pay someone to humiliate and laugh at me. The tapes of being bullied throughout my formative schooling years had led me to a lifetime of self-ridicule. I learned how to beat myself up better than they ever had. Even today, some of those words haunt me.

I finally went to see the dietician and I'm so grateful I did. She didn't teach me anything I didn't already know, but she did become a vital player in my weight loss; she became my first cheerleader. I also followed through with my surgery pre-op appointment. The nurse in the gastro office informed me that I qualified for the surgery, but I would have to prove over a six-month period that I could follow a diet plan and become healthier. I asked if it was possible to lose enough weight to no longer qualify for the surgery. She told me that at my current Body Mass Index (BMI) of 33, it would not be possible to get under the 28 BMI requirement in six months. I thanked her, because in that moment, she gave me a gift; I now had a goal.

Sometime during my fourth month of weight loss, I was no longer dieting; something had changed in how I naturally lived my life and I didn't have to try as hard to eat healthily. My body had started craving the good food and when it didn't, it only took a bite to satisfy me again. My health was at risk and I didn't want my children to be motherless. I had gained a voice, a piece of self-worth, a morsel of self-satisfaction. I can't give specifics of what changed; I can't tell you that I started pumping iron or working out crazily; none of those things happened. I did work out for thirty minutes almost every morning on the Wii Fit. I ate proper portions and began walking more. It wasn't that I was suddenly trying. It was that the desire to heal my body and mind had finally found its hold on my heart. I discovered the missing connection. Losing weight became a side effect.

I overcame my first challenge at the six-month mark. When the nurse called back for my next surgery appointment, I proudly told her I had successfully lost seventy pounds—enough weight to no longer qualify for the surgery. The extra pounds magically vanished, and I no longer engaged in stress eating. That was until a gentleman at the store noticed me. He smiled and said hi, and while I knew he was simply being friendly, I reeled into a familiar, dark place. I lost my shield and I was no longer invisible. Thankfully, I remained in therapy, because the next weeks would prove challenging.

What is often lacking in weight loss programs is a hard look at how and why people put on the weight in the first place. It took weeks for me to realize that my weight had become a shield against men's gazes, their unwanted advances, comments, and lewd behavior—better to be fat than wanted. Not long after I hit puberty and lost all of my baby fat, I was raped. My added weight not only became a shield, it gave me a false sense of security. I felt invisible when I was heavier, and in being invisible, I felt safer. If they can't see you, they can't hurt you. There was also a part of me that believed if someone tried to hurt me, I could stop them because I was bigger, heavier. If nothing else, I could sit on them. My weight made me miserable, but it also protected me.

I still have moments of fear and anxiety. It's not that I never stress eat anymore; instead, I have learned to limit what and how much I eat. I haven't had to fight to stay thinner; it happens because much of my life has truly changed. A year ago, I started T'ai Chi. It has been a tremendous help. Also, I took up bike riding a month ago—something I never thought I'd do again.

Recently, I overcame one of my final weight challenges. I became overweight. You might wonder, "What? How is that good?" When you start at morbidly obese and move to simply being overweight, it becomes a celebration. I still have weight to lose, but I'm no longer actively trying to lose weight. Instead, I'm learning to be happy and healthy.

The best news is that I went from stage four kidney failure down to stage three. My nephrologist was right—only I could change my life and my future. You can, too. You can become bigger than the bullies and the rapists. You can heal your mind, and your body will follow, if you allow it. It doesn't mean you never have eating setbacks, but instead of eating the cake, you only eat the piece.

What people sometimes forget is that you don't have to do it alone. There are people out there who can, and will, help. All you need to do is ask. Everyone's struggle is different, yet at our core, we are all the same. You can face the hard work and challenges, because you've faced worse and you're still here, still kicking. Find your voice, your passion, your zest for life, and overcome the pain of your past. You are the only one who can do it.

I love that I'm a mother, a daughter, a sister, a grandma, a wife, an aunt, and a friend, but I've lived all my life defined by roles I play or the sicknesses I have. I write to free my being, my desires, my self. I long to just be.

65 POWER POUCH BY GRETCHEN YONKO

My body isn't just mine. My children each own a piece. They know when I strut my mama stuff around the house that it means I'm ecstatic about their existence.

My pre-everything-breaking-loose, ten-year-old daughter tells me that her sleepover friend thinks my shirts are HUGE. Well yah, compared to a ten-year-old's. Does this really need to be pointed out? I snort and remind my female child I need gigantic shirts, for these humongous shirts need to fit over HER power pouch.

"My power pouch?" She tilts her head and squints in an attempt to connect my words to what she is learning about "good" bodies from friends, internet, school teachers, neighbors, her dad, her dad's girlfriend, her dad's girlfriend's mom, her dad's girlfriend's teenage sons, and her grandpa, grandma, abuelita, oma, opa, cousins, ads and billboards. So many perfect bodies on ads and billboards.

"Yah," I smile back, with my voluminous chest thrust out as I pick up, with two hands, the grabbable skin and fat plopping over my upper pubes. It obscures my view for shaving, so I usually don't bother. "My power pouch; it attaches to me right at the scar left by the cut through which you were thrust into the bright light.

You decided last minute that, if you had to come out at all, you wanted to come out a new hole made just for you. My body above the scar just stayed this way. It reminds me of you. Your big brain pushed through the layers of tissue, muscle, fat, and skin, anointing it with power. I wear this part of me with pride. You changed my life. My body created a monument to you; my power pouch."

"But mom," her little brother chimes in, "what did I do?" His eyes wide and expectant, wishing to stake a claim. If he wasn't a little boy, but a man on a date, I would have rolled my eyes hard enough to flip dice.

"Oh, my dear, I remember you every time I sneeze." I wink and start to walk toward the kitchen, still wearing my coat after returning from work. I drop it on the stool so I can take out the frozen chicken that I forgot to put in the fridge to thaw. As usual, every time I stop or change course in the kitchen, my son bumps into me. He always keeps close. A few years earlier, he would come up to me while at the stove, wrap his arms around my waist as far as he could, rest his head on my butt, and exclaim that I had a nice soft pillow to rest on. I'm curious how things will play out if he carries that into adulthood and tries it on a lady, if he is inclined toward the ladies. But this time he was bursting with a request, too Tigger-y to relax.

"Mom, why do you remember me when you sneeze?"

"Sometimes when I cough, too. Because you, too, have a big brain, Honey. You chose the traditional route into the world. But that melon of yours was a little bigger than your mama was ready for just then. I didn't really bounce back totally. You too changed me forever." My smile seems to calm the beginnings of a brow furrow. We don't need to get into the details and I know it will only add to the misconception that the vaginal opening is a pee hole, but it just is what it is. Mama is now incontinent. It is a direct result of his fifteen-inch head. So, it is. "You ripped me a bit as you left the comfort of the power pouch, and now when I sneeze, some pee leaks out. I can't hold it in no matter how hard I try. So, I remember you, my little watermelon." He visually loads this information into that gargantuan head of his and I fully expect a comment the next time I sneeze.

My dates don't know about my son's contribution to my body, but they sure can't miss my daughter's.

My power pouch, the grabbable, lovable blob of me. Not one has questioned it. Not one man has been noticeably disgusted by it. Not one man has followed the advice of all those beauty product advertisers and shunned the woman before him because she didn't use their products. Because who would question a woman with a power pouch? There is no discussion. No apology needs to be made for it. Accept it or miss out on the double bonus, grabbable skin blobs next shelf up; the other part of my body forever changed by having babies. Ka Pow!

Gretchen Yonko is a middle-aged, Midwestern mom who still rounds up when asked her age. She likes her "used-to" and "still-going-to" life. Her current status as a single, government accountant at a university in Menomonie, Wisconsin might be temporary. Until she knows otherwise, she enjoys what comes her way.

ACKNOWLEDGMENTS

When I planned this book, it was meant to be far slimmer—a collection of perhaps ten writers' thoughts on the conundrum of being a woman with a body, a face, a closetful of clothes—but it grew well beyond my imaginings.

The quality of the submissions the women sent in for *Women Under Scrutiny* stunned me. Honest. Luminous. Disturbing. Blunt. Artistic. In the end, the envisioned ten grew to well over sixty, and for that I am grateful. I thank every woman who contributed. You inspired me.

Nancy MacDonald's editing and management of *Women Under Scrutiny* brought this book to a level I could never have achieved without her. She is indefatigable, dedicated, smart, kept me on track, and loved the contributors as much as I did. She made this book.

Kathleen Lynch of Black Kat Design: thank you for your way-beyond-expected help in this project. I came to you for the cover and ended up in love with you for catching the enthusiasm the contributors engendered.

Carolyn Ring: Wow, am I lucky to have found you! When I'm in any sort of pickle—whether it be technical, graphic, or a myriad of 'other,' you have the answer; —and what a pleasure you are to work with!

Ann-Marie Nieves, Stephanie Abou, MJ Rose, Kathy Crowley, Nichole Bernier, Ginny DeLuca, Juliette Fay, and EB Moore: You help me get through every day of writing.

Family: Sara, Becca, Jason, Jill, Jesse, Bruce & Jean, thank you for pretending that I don't spill all over the page every day. Most of all, thank you for being my light and love.

And Jeff, thank you for everything. Really. Everything. Your love made me accept me for the first time.

ABOUT RANDY SUSAN MEYERS

The drama of Randy Susan Meyers' internationally bestselling novels is informed by over twenty years working with families impacted by emotional and physical violence. Her career has included working with batterers and victims of domestic violence, overseeing educational, recreational, and social programs for the City of Boston, overseeing and directing a community center in Mission Hill, Boston—as well as jobs running the gamut from bartender to wringing out dripping wet hot sheets in a tie-dye factory.

Waisted, her newest novel, which inspired **Women Under Scrutiny**, begins with these lines:

Everyone hated a fat woman, but none more than she hated herself. Alice knew this to be true. Today's proof? She, along with six other substantial women, stood in the parking lot avoiding each other, as though their abundance of flesh might transfer from body to body, despite all waiting to board the bus for the same reason: "the unique opportunity to spend an entire month exploring ways to bring yourself into balance."

Early pre-publication praise for **Waisted** includes:

To Alice and Daphne, being thin is taking over their world. They become fast friends when they both sign up for a program promising dramatic weight loss in one month. Meyers exquisitely explores body image, family, and marriage in this surprisingly deep novel. though she starts with a fictionalized version of the TV show *The Biggest Loser*, she dips into major issues of race, culture, obsession, and sisterhood. Taking on the timely topic of how a woman is perceived in today's society, she twists it into how far women will go to be what society deems right, and at what cost—a marriage, a family obligation, a personal goal? A compelling story that will leave readers giving their scale the side eye.

—Booklist

"Meyers spins a compelling tale, raising critical questions about familial, social, and cultural messages about body image..."

—Kirkus Reviews

"Meyers delivers a timely examination of body image, family, friendship, and what it means to be a woman in modern society. It will appeal to anyone who has ever dreaded stepping on a scale; even those who haven't will learn from it. Culturally inclusive and societally on point, this is a must-read."

—Library Journal

"Suspenseful. Witty. Warm. Wonderful. Disturbing. Thought-ful. Compelling. Riveting. Seriously important. Inspiring. It made me hungry. Then made me never want to eat again. I recognized myself. Then hated myself. Then loved myself. This is a must read for every woman who ever stepped on the scale with her eyes closed. And every woman who hasn't."

—**M.J. Rose,** *New York Times* bestselling
author of *Tiffany Blues*

"*Waisted* is a big-hearted triumph of a novel. Meyers tackles painful truths and thorny issues while weaving a smart and engaging story about weight loss, self-acceptance and the forti-fying power of female friendship."

—**Carolyn Parkhurst,** *New York Times* bestselling
author of *Harmony* and *The Dogs of Babel*

Meyers' previous novel, **The Widow of Wall Street**, described by *Publisher's Weekly* as "An engaging and sharp reflection of the rapid changes in marital dynamics over the course of the 20th century, as well as a cautionary tale about the dangers and allure of ambition in the heyday of Wall Street," was a PopSugar Pick, a Refinery 29 Pick, a *New York Post* "Must Read Book," and one of New York Subway's "New York Stories." *Associated Press* called the novel "compelling."

Meyers' earlier novels, **The Murderer's Daughters** and **Accidents of Marriage** were chosen as "Must Read Books" by the Massachusetts Center for the Book, who wrote, "The clear and distinctive voice of Randy Susan Meyers will have you enraptured and wanting more." ***The Murderer's Daughters***, deemed a "Knock-out Debut" by the *LA Times* was a nationwide Target Book Club pick.

The Boston Globe called Meyers' second novel, ***The Comfort of Lies*** "Sharp and biting, and sometimes wickedly funny when the author skewers Boston's class and neighborhood dividing lines, but it has a lot of heart, too."

Choosing ***Accidents of Marriage*** as a *People* "Pick of The Week," the magazine wrote, "This novel's unsparing look at emotional abuse and its devastating consequences gives it gravity and bite, while a glimpse into a physically damaged mind both surprises and fascinates."

Meyers lives in Boston with her husband. She teaches at Boston's Grub Street Writers' Center and at Writers in Progress in Northampton, MA.

You can learn more at: www.randysusanmeyers.com.

*WAISTED, Published by Atria Books/Simon &
Schuster. Cover design by Ella Laytham*

ABOUT ROSIE'S PLACE

I've supported Rosie's Place in Boston since they opened. Rosie's Place exemplifies social justice, community working together, and women helping women, and I dedicate this book to Kip Tiernan—Rosie's Place founder. I am thrilled to donate the profits from *Women Under Scrutiny* to Rosie's Place.

"Rosie's Place was founded when, in 1974, our founder Kip Tiernan saw poor women disguising themselves as men to get a meal at men-only shelters in Boston and said, "We can do better than that." Our mission is to provide a safe and nurturing environment that helps poor and homeless women maintain their

dignity, seek opportunity and find security in their lives. We continue to reach out to poor and homeless women who hide in plain sight, trying every day to understand the right way to encourage and engage them.

We acknowledge that coming to Rosie's Place is for most of our guests an admission of defeat. For her, that first day in our community is probably one of her worst days. She arrives considering herself a collection of problems, of faults—homeless, hungry, jobless, addicted, ill. Right from the start, we work to turn that around, to hold in our hearts the image of a strong and dignified woman who can make decisions that help her go where she wants to go. While we provide resources and information, we also provide the message that every woman is a resilient and resourceful individual, whose past and present need not be her limits. We strive to hold that image regardless of the setbacks our guests face along the way.

Rosie's Place opened its doors 45 years ago as the first women-only shelter in the U.S. Today, we not only provide meals and shelter but also create answers for 12,000 women a year through wide-ranging support, housing and education services. Rosie's Place relies solely on the generous support of individuals, foundations and corporations and does not accept any city, state or federal funding. Thanks to these donations, 87 cents of every dollar raised goes directly to services for poor and homeless women." —from Rosie's Place website

Donations to Rosie's Place can be made at rosiesplace.org

NOTES

35. Alumni of Weight Programs by Heather Clift

1. As of this writing, a member must be 13 to join. The full policy can be found on the Weight Watcher website.